CLASSIC
WHITTLING

BASIC TECHNIQUES
AND
OLD-TIME PROJECTS

RICK WIEBE

LINDEN PUB

Classic Whittling
Basic Techniques and Old-Time Projects
by Rick Wiebe

© Rick Wiebe
Linden Publishing, Inc.
2006 S. Mary
Fresno, CA 93721
www.lindenpub.com
ISBN: 978-1-61035-254-3

Linden Publishing titles may be purchased in quantity at special discounts
for educational, business, or promotional use. To inquire about discount
pricing, please refer to the contact information below. For permission to use
any portion of this book for academic purposes, please contact the
Copyright Clearance Center at www.copyright.com.

Printed in the United States of America
35798642

Library of Congress Cataloging-in-Publication Data

Wiebe, Rick, author.
    Classic whittling : basic techniques and old-time projects / Rick Wiebe.
        pages cm
    Includes index.
    ISBN 978-1-61035-254-3 (pbk. : alk. paper)
    1. Wood-carving. I. Title.
    TT199.7.W534 2015
    736'.4--dc23
                                        2015026575

Contents

Introduction

Got a knife?

You probably do, and have this book in your hands because you want to use it.

If you don't have one you need to get at least one soon. An old Finnish proverb says "a knifeless man is a lifeless man." The Finns have it right in my opinion, and would surely apply the saying to people of both genders. Everyone needs a knife that they can carry with them and use for a myriad of things pretty much every day.

Whittlers, of course, need a knife for their craft as well as for the everyday tasks that are so much simpler when a sharp blade is available. When you get a good knife, get it sharp, and begin to learn to use it, you will make an amazing discovery, a knife is actually a magic wand. With it you can turn ordinary sticks and small pieces of wood that might otherwise be burned or thrown away, into useful, enjoyable and even artistic objects and have fun doing it. Junk to art. Trash to usefulness, firewood to fun—sounds like magic to me!

That is what this book is all about, teaching you how to wave the wand, so to speak, and have a great time doing it.

I speak from considerable experience in this line, having been whittlin' for over 60 years now, with no intention of stopping. It was fun when I was a kid, and a young person. As the years went by I enjoyed making things for other people and in time my own children, and now my grandchildren. For many years I have been teaching a lot of people how to experience this craft. Some have been

quite young and some have been getting on in years, and they have all discovered an activity that can bring immense satisfaction.

I have found that even people whom, for whatever reason, are not in the process of doing this activity, are still interested to see it going on. If I whittle in a public place, (I often whittle little gifts for servers in restaurants while waiting for my food, or on ferries etc.), it is rare that I don't get a good conversation going with someone that I have never met before. People are fascinated by the magic! They ask a lot of questions, about the wood, the knife, how to sharpen how long I've been doing it and other things too.

Whittlin' isn't just for old guys. It is a lifetime activity. It isn't expensive, and it is safe. Yes, cuts happen, but no one is in any danger of drowning or broken bones or debilitating sports injuries. The only time an ambulance has attended one of my classes, so far, was when someone sat on a bee and had an allergic reaction. Compared with activities like bicycling, swimming and skiing, whittlin' is absurdly safe.

It is very a portable hobby and one that fits in with a lot of other activities. It really goes with camping, but all kinds of other things lend themselves to the occasional whittlin' fit too. In fact my hand is kind of twitching right now. Maybe yours is too. So let's start!

CHAPTER ONE
Tools & Equipment
or Choose Your Wand

Whittlin' is just carving while using a knife as the main or only tool. Other kinds of carving use a variety of tools including many hand tools and sometimes power tools of various kinds. Whittlers mostly stick with knives, though sometimes a few other simple cutting tools are used too.

A basic tool that is used often by whittlers is a pocket knife, which folds up and fits safely in a pocket or bag when not in use, but is quickly available when a whittlin' fit strikes. For most people a simple folding knife between 3¼ and 4" long when closed will do the job. There is no need for all kinds of gadgets on the knife, and mostly locks are not necessary either, though there are some knives on which they are useful. Knives need to be small enough so that they are not clumsy but large enough to provide a good and non-cramping grip.

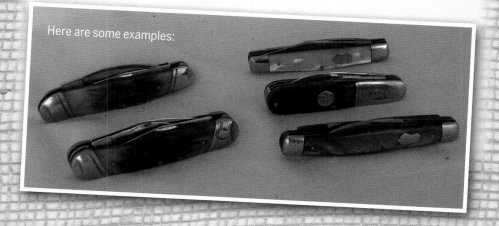

Here are some examples:

This is called a Barlow knife, and similar ones are made by several manufacturers. It is a great knife for anyone, only 3⅜" long, though some companies make them bigger and call them Daddy or even Granddaddy Barlows. This is a good knife for whittlin' just the way it is—well except for sharpening which will be covered in the next chapter.

Here's one with a slightly different handle material, and modified blades. Blades can be easily modified using files.

This one is a single bladed locking knife made in France called an Opinel. They are made in many sizes. A #7 or 8 will do the job for most whittlers, especially if they are modified as shown (below).

The handles can be modified to suit the individual too.

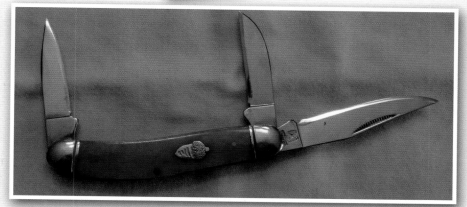

This is a Sowbelly Stockman knife that has been modified.

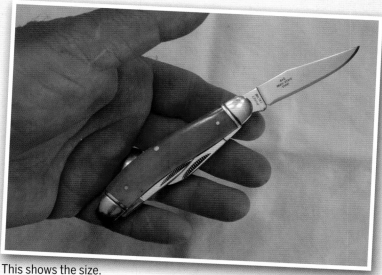

This shows the size.

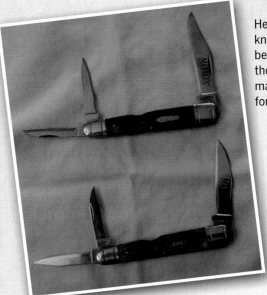

Here are two identical knives, one of which has been modified more than the other. These two are man-sized knives. Too big for kids.

Here are a few fixed blade knives (non-folding) that are useful for whittlin'. The top one is a factory made whittlin' knife made in Switzerland by a company called Pfeil (pronounced "file"), that makes very fine carving tools. The bottom three are knives made using Swedish laminated steel blanks made by Mora. I made the handles.

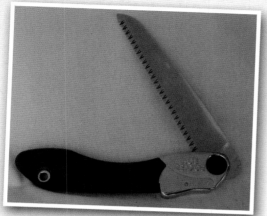

This is a device that will save a lot of work and isn't too bulky. It is called a Silky Saw. It folds for carrying, and has amazingly good and fast cutting teeth. Every whittler who sees one in action wants one!

This is an old gouge. Very useful for—well, gouging! It is a tool that is used a lot by carvers, who often have dozens of them in different sizes and degrees of sweep. Spoon whittlers will find it almost essential. It is OK to buy old gouges, but refrain from buying cheap gouges. They will drive you nuts. Unless you are finding an old or maybe just a not so old but used one at a sale, any gouge selling for less than about $25.00 is not worth owning. Period. The specific depth and width of the gouge is not critical for whittlers, but it should be at least ½" (12 mm) wide to be of use for spoon work.

This one which could be used instead of the one above, is called a palm gouge because of the style of handle. Unlike the previous gouge, this one is not designed to be struck with a mallet. This one is a little flatter, not so much gouge, and a little smaller in width, but still very useful for a whittler who would like to make spoons. Unlike the first gouge, this one is not an antique.

This is a palm gouge that is designed to get way down into the bottom of a bowl, ladle or cup. It is known by carvers as a spoon gouge or as a short bent gouge. Whittlers who want to make ladles, bowls or cups will find it almost indispensable. It should be no smaller than 10 mm, a little less than ½". These last two palm gouges will cost at least $25.00 each. If you get ones costing less prepare to be disappointed.

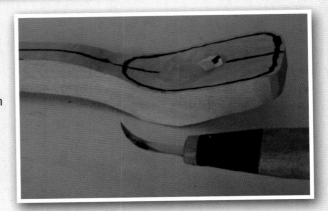

Here is a traditional spoon whittlers tool called a bent, or crooked knife. It works, but in my opinion, not nearly as well as the gouges for whittlin' purposes.

There are of course a few other items that will be of use for whittlers, such as pencils, and tape. Things that almost everyone has anyway.

Glue is useful at times, and there are lots of different kinds. An extremely useful product is medium viscosity, gap filling, cynoacralate glue and the accelerator that goes with it. This is available at hobby shops that sell flying model aircraft kits.

Hot glue is useful for some projects. You probably have a hot glue gun already.

A wood burning pen can be useful too, as can various paints, felt pens and the like, but these items are not necessary to have fun with this craft.

If you are going to process your own wood from logs, saplings or trees, larger saws, even chainsaws, axes, and machetes will be useful too.

The knife though, is the main tool, and you can do amazing things with just a knife or two.

Oh yes, you will need some items to make and keep that knife sharp, and that's the subject for the next chapter.

Many whittlers these days find that using a cut resistant glove on the hand not holding the knife saves some blood. In my whittlin' classes for kids, all of the students have to wear a protective glove on their non-knife hand. I have applied a lot fewer band aids since establishing this policy, but I am concerned sometimes that the use of the glove may lead to carelessness that could cause problems when no glove is available. These gloves are not cut proof, but cut resistant. They are not even a little poke resistant. To get that kind of protection would be so cumbersome as to be useless.

Here is a glove with stainless steel in it that can be found at fishing supply stores as a "Filleting glove". It works well as a whittler's glove especially if some liquid silicone rubber is applied to the palm and fingers and allowed to harden. The rubber will remain flexible and assist in the grip on the wood.

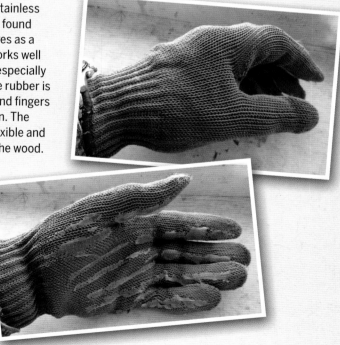

Another approach is to get a glove like this made of Kevlar. Bulletproof vests are made with Kevlar.

Be sure the glove has leather stitched to the inside of the fingers and palm. The leather helps with the grip and also provides a little puncture protection. Carving gloves provide good protection from slicing type cuts, but very little protection from poking, which is worth keeping in mind when using them. Remember that you are not immune from cuts when wearing a glove. Taping the thumb of the knife holding hand, can help prevent injury when whittlers use what I call "the potato peeler cut," and most whittlers use that cut a lot. Some just build up a protective thumb guard out of masking tape or duct tape and that works. Others use a product called "Vetwrap" that is available at stores that sell horse supplies. Still others learn to carve without protective devices.

A lap board is kind of a portable work bench that sits on a whittler's lap. It can be very useful, providing a surface to cut down on that will not destroy the knife edge, while protecting the clothes and legs of the whittler. It provides a good place to lay an extra knife, or pencil or anything else that needs to be kept within reach. Unless the whittlin' is very enthusiastic, it might even catch some chips!

This is a "lap board". I saw another whittler using one of these at the carving show in Mesa, AZ, and got inspired to make one. There was some used wood that was lying around so I just thought a bit and made one that works for me.

These photos will help you make one too, if you want.

Here it is in use. It provides something to hold the wood against when cutting, and catches a lot of chips and shavings.

This is a lot safer than cutting down on your leg! I also made a divider so that tools, pencils, snacks etc., can be segregated from most of the wood shavings.

This view shows how the vertical pieces on the underside of the board provide stability as the legs brace against them. I have seen some made with some carpet scraps attached to the underside too.

The lap board is handy as long as it is nearby, but often I am nowhere near my lap board and still do a lot of whittlin', so don't get tied to your stuff and be kind of out of action when you aren't near your home workshop. Just remember to take your knife, and you can whittle almost anywhere.

CHAPTER TWO
Sharpening

If you can already get a knife sharp enough that it will easily shave the hair off your arm, you may not need this chapter. For most people however, this could be the most important part of this book. Sharpening is without doubt the most important part of whittlin'. If your knife isn't sharp, you will struggle. If it is really sharp you can concentrate on making fine cuts and doing good work.

It is possible, by the way, to do much of the work in this book using what is called a "utility knife" either in the folding or non-folding versions. These knives have pre-sharpened replaceable blades, and people using them really don't need to know about sharpening. They can be purchased at any hardware or building supply store. I find them clumsy for my work though, and think you really should learn to sharpen a regular knife.

It is important to read and understand this chapter first and then actually sharpen several knives until you "get" this before you attempt much whittlin'.

To sharpen a knife like the ones in the chapter on tools, you will need a sharpening stone. There are several options here. In the photos I am using an aluminium oxide stone. It works well, and isn't very expensive.

Some people like to use devices that are flat like sharpening stones, but have nickel plated steel surfaces with diamond particles imbedded in them. These are often referred to as "Diamond Stones". Diamonds do a great job of grinding steel. These items are more expensive than the aluminium oxide stone, but not as much more as you might think. If you decide to try them, make sure you get one that is called "fine"—with about 1000 grit. Some amazingly effective diamond "stones" can be obtained for very little money at discount tool stores. The main drawback to them is that they do not come in very fine grits.

It is also possible to get "wet or dry" sandpaper, cut it into 2" wide strips and glue (with regular wood glue—not hot glue) them to flat pieces of wood and make your own "stone". Actually, you can make several, some coarse out of 220 grit, some medium ones out of 440 grit and some fine out of 800 or 1000 grit. Grit sizes do not have to be exactly as listed. This works well, but the sandpaper wears out fairly quickly and needs to be replaced. The advantage of the sandpaper is that it is available in almost any builder's supply, and in places that have items designed for automotive painting.

A good, and inexpensive solution if you can't find an aluminium oxide stone of about 600 to 800 grit, might be to get the inexpensive diamond products for preliminary work on new or really dull blades and then make a fine "stone" with 1000 grit wet or dry sandpaper for finishing. A good choice for the aluminium oxide stone is Norton's IB8.

I do not recommend using Japanese water stones. They will work, but they are expensive and require maintenance.

The various gizmos that people put knives into and pull them through are mostly useless for whittlers. Avoid them.

Never attempt to sharpen a knife on an electric grinder that has a grey/black wheel. Unless you are a real expert, you will ruin the blade of your knife. There are power sharpening systems that are OK and work, but most of them are too expensive and unnecessary for whittlers who just want to sharpen a couple of knives.

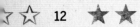

It is kind of a fuss to get all this together, but take the time to do it and as you learn to sharpen and get really good, you will find that it really was all worth it.

Remember to read this whole chapter before you start actually sharpening. There is something else that you will need to get that will be mentioned later.

OK. Get your stone. If you have a fairly coarse stone start with it and repeat the stone work until you have worked though all your grits—or you could just use a 600 or 800 grit for all of your stone work. Remember, the bigger the number the finer the grit.

If you are using an IB8 Norton you need to put some oil on the stone. Baby oil is mineral oil and it is far less expensive than other kinds of oil. If you are using an aluminium oxide stone that didn't come oily, use some water with a tiny bit of dishwashing soap in it. If a diamond stone, use it with the baby oil or dry. Sandpaper—water or dry.

The angle of the blade on the stone is important (**Photo 1**). Too steep, and even if the edge is sharp it won't go through the wood very well. Too flat and the edge will fold or chip. I have found that about 10 degrees works well. For most pocket knives, a nickel on the stone

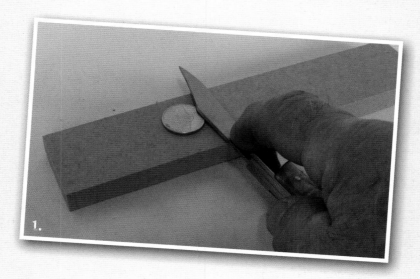

1.

2.

can help. Tip up the back of the blade until the nickel will just fit, and that should be about the right angle.

In my classes I give everyone a little wooden wedge cut to a 10 degree angle in place of the nickel (**Photo 2**). The nickel, or the wedge, does not move back and forth on the stone. Whichever one you use is just there for you to check your angle from time to time to ensure that you are doing it right.

Hold the knife on the stone as shown in Photos 1 and 2. Put some pressure down on it and move it back and forth. Make the strokes as long as is possible and comfortable to you. If you prefer to move the blade in a sort of circular motion that is OK too. As you do this the abrasive of the stone will grind away a tiny bit of steel. Try to do the entire edge from base to tip. If using oil or water on the stone, keep it wet. Don't rush. Keep the pressure on and maintain the correct angle. Go slowly enough that you can see what you are doing. After maybe 75 or so strokes, take a look at the part you have been grinding on. It probably will look like this (**Photo 3**). If the entire side of the knife is scratched, don't worry. You haven't ruined it, but you have let the blade go flat on the stone. Try again, and maintain that 10 degree angle.

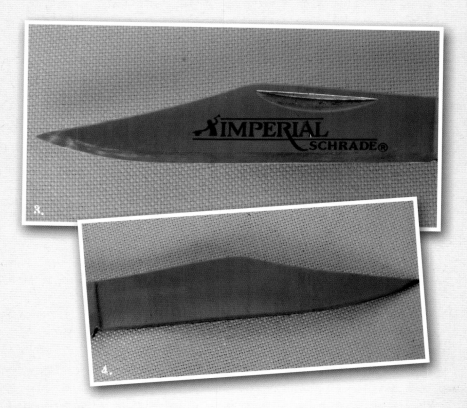

By the way, don't be afraid of wrecking your knife. It is extremely unlikely that you will. And even if you did, but learned to really sharpen in the process, it would be worth it.

If you compare the side that you have been grinding on to the one that you haven't touched there will be a difference (**Photo 4**). See how much narrower the factory bevel is.

Run your finger gently from the blade spine to the edge on the side of the knife that you did *not* grind on (**Photo 5**). If you can feel a little "hook" of steel turned over by the stone, you are on the right track. Keep working on the stone on the first side of the knife, always at the correct angle until you can feel this little hook—called a "wire edge"—all the way along the blade, not just in one or two places. Do not start grinding on the other side of the blade until you

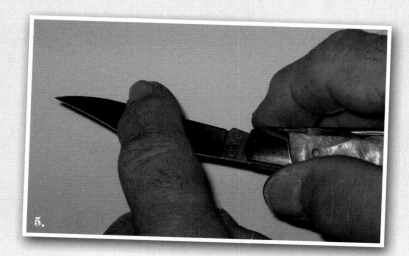

have achieved the wire edge on the first side. Remember, the wire edge forms on the side of the blade that is not touching the stone,

It is not possible to over emphasize the importance of this wire edge or what some people call a burr. If you do not get the wire edge, you will never get the knife really sharp. So don't be tempted to fudge here.

Once you have the wire edge, then and only then, turn the knife over and using the same angle do the other side of the blade until the wire edge forms on the side that now is not in contact with the stone. This edge is absolutely vital to the sharpening process. The wire edge must be formed on both sides of the blade while the blade is worked at the correct angle on the stone. Of course, it is not possible to have the wire edge on both sides of the blade at the same time. It will get pushed over by the stone to the side that is not in contact with the stone. Remember to keep a fair bit of pressure on while doing the rubbing.

I know you want to hurry up and get to the cutting part, but this is honestly the most important thing you can learn about whittlin'.

6.

Now, if you have some finer grit to use, start the grinding process again on the first side of the blade, putting the most recent wire edge down on the stone, and raise the wire edges both ways again.

When you have raised the wire edge both ways on your finest stone, put the most recent wire edge down on the stone again, and give it a few light rubs at the correct angle. Then flip it over and give it a few light rubs on the other side. Then back to the first side and a few more. Go back and forth like this 4 or 5 times. Now it should be difficult to feel the wire edge on either side.

We're not quite done yet, but we are getting there. If you have raised the wire edge on both sides of the blade, and all along the blade, and you have honed it mostly all off, while maintaining the correct angle all the while, you are right on the verge of having a shaving sharp blade.

Now you need a strop.

You can make one easily. An old belt glued to a stick with the inside up works well, or a piece of denim (**Photo 6**) from an old pair of blue jeans, glued to a stick, works just as well. Size isn't all that important, but to start somewhere, make it 1½–2" wide and 12–16" long.

The strop needs some extremely fine buffing compound on it to work. In the photo (**Photo 7**) I am putting on a cream product called *Rick's White Lightnin'*. If you can't get this, you can go to a discount tool store and get a stick of green or white buffing compound and use it like a crayon to color your strop. Do not use red jeweller's rouge. It doesn't work because it is designed for soft metals like silver and gold, not steel.

The compound goes all over the strop (**Photo 8**).

The cream needs to dry for a few minutes; the crayoned on product can be used right away. By the way the amount seen on this strop will sharpen at least 100 blades before more needs to be applied.

9.

Now lay your blade on the strop, at that 10-degree angle and with quite a bit of pressure, pull the blade in one direction only—with the edge trailing (**Photo 9**). Do not change the angle for the entire stroke and do not give it a little flip at the end. Actually it is a good idea to put the little wedge or the nickel at the end of the strop so that you can kind of aim for the right angle and finish at the guide.

Do this about 100 times, working your way across the blade as you go, so that the entire length of the blade winds up getting stropped, though the whole blade will not be stropped on every stroke. And yes you do have to do the 100 strokes. Then turn the knife over and strop the other side 100 times.

The strop is black because the buffing compound has worn off some steel from the blade, and nearly microscopic steel particles appear black. Black goop will also accumulate on sharpening stones as they are used.

If you have carefully followed these instructions, your knife will be sharper than it ever has been before. You will be able to do good work with it.

To keep it sharp, strop it 20 times or so per side when you notice it needs a bit. The edge will come back, if it hasn't been damaged.

If the blade gets nicked, or you cut something you shouldn't, you will need to go back to the stone and get the wire edges.

Well that is work! It is enough work that whittlers get kind of paranoid about their edges. They don't cut dirty wood, because dirt is grit and grit are tiny stones and that wreck the edge, and then its back to the sharpening process. They cannot comprehend the idea of sticking their knife in the ground (instant dull—every time). If someone wants to borrow their knife, the answer is, "What would you like *me* to cut for you," because non-whittlers often do unspeakable things with knives; scrape gum off shoes, open cans, use them to pry lids off, or, use them as a screw driver! Always reserve the right to say, "My knife is never used for that."

People who are not used to really sharp knives can hurt themselves. Many years ago, I stupidly loaned my knife a couple of times, and both times the borrowers wound up in emergency rooms.

Pay attention! Sharp knives can cut you. They can also do a lot of great work. Let's do some.

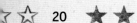

CHAPTER THREE

Finding Whittlin' Material

The basic material for whittlin' is, well kind of obviously, wood. There are other possible materials too, which we will talk about later, but most whittlers pretty much stick to wood.

Sometimes I have had people ask me, "Is that some kind special stuff you are working with or just ordinary wood?" Lets be clear about the fact that there is no such thing as "ordinary wood." There are many different species of trees and each of them has different wood. Some are good for whittlin', some are kind of OK, and some are horrible and really not much fun. Some are very soft and easy to cut, and some kinds of wood are difficult to cut. Some are so hard that whittlin' them with a knife is close to impossible.

Some whittlers love to carve certain types of wood that others can't stand, and some use a particular kind of wood because it is what grows close to where they live. For example, I love to carve birch into spoons, ladles and cups. It grows where I live and so it is easy to obtain. It does not grow in southern California, though, and unless whittlers there get some shipped or brought to them they will have to find something else.

In today's world, it is possible to buy almost any species of wood if you try hard enough and spend enough. Part of the craft of whittlin' though is to use what is available, and in most places there is some kind of wood available that will work for something, though it might be necessary to buy wood for some projects.

Wood is not really that expensive to buy, and I would recommend that beginning whittlers especially should make every effort and even spend a bit to get the best wood possible. It will make success with projects more likely.

There is no wood that is good for every project. For example, basswood, sometimes-called linden, white pine, and sugar pine are great for carving animal and human figures, but not so good for carving spoons. Birch is great for spoons, but most carvers would not choose it for human caricatures. Some experimentation is necessary to find what you like to carve.

Don't be afraid to try some kind of wood that you encounter. You might find a new favorite, or you might find a new kind of firewood! I often say that what I am doing is just producing "designer firewood" anyway.

A complicating factor is that some trees/wood go by different names in different places. For example trembling aspen is called white poplar in some places and popple in others. Or worse, sometimes the same name is used to describe different wood as in the case of red cedar. In eastern and southern North America what is called red cedar (and is not bad as a carving wood), is a totally different tree and wood from what is called red cedar in the West. Western red cedar is not a good carving wood at all, especially for beginners.

All of this means that whittlers need to learn something about trees and how to recognize different ones and especially to recognize the ones that will be useful for the projects that they wish to do. This has never been easier to do, with all kinds of information available on the Internet.

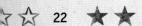

Following are some woods to use and some to avoid. Don't be offended if I don't like one that you think is great.

Good for whittlin':

Eastern white pine.
Western white pine.
Basswood.
Trembling aspen.
Tulip poplar.
Birch.
Willow. There are a lot of different kinds.
Huon pine (in Australia).
Jelutong.
Butternut.
Walnut. Several nut trees have usable wood.
Pecan.
Buckeye. Horse chestnut is either the same or very similar.
Honduras and African mahogany.
Philippine mahogany is useful for some things—not so great for others.
Spruce—for some things.
Some types of **maple** are good, some very hard.
Alder can often be a good substitute for birch. It can even be found in some places in Southern California.
Yellow cedar. Sometimes called Alaskan cedar, and cypress—different than the bald cypress that grows in the southern US.
Ponderosa pine is good for big, bold projects but not so good for small ones.
Sugar pine.
Some carvers like to use **cottonwood** (black poplar) and many love to whittle cottonwood bark.
Eastern white cedar.
Some **fir** trees, but not Douglas fir which is not true fir.
Hazel—makes good walking sticks.

I would suggest that whittlers would do well to avoid:

Really hard woods like **hard maple, beech,** and **hickory,** though they have their applications. If you need to whittle an axe handle, there is nothing better than hickory.

Western red cedar—it crushes and splits far too easily but makes great kindling.

Monterey pine, called radiata pine sometimes.

Southern yellow pine—hard stuff.

Balsa—has its applications but too crushy.

Douglas fir—called Oregon pine in some places.

Larch.

Tamarack.

Hemlock.

Apple wood—some types are very hard.

Many of the **fruit trees** are quite hard, but try them anyway you might find one you like.

Red, white, and black live oak. Some oaks are good to carve with the proper tools, but not great for knife whittlin'.

Madrone—called arbutus in Canada. Very hard, though it can be used.

Lodgepole pine. If nothing else is available OK.

Dogwood—far too hard.

And there are hundreds more kinds of wood that can be tried. Have fun with this!

If you buy wood, either know what you are buying or consult people who do. People who work in big box stores usually do not know the difference between white pine, spruce, lodgepole pine and hemlock. Consult speciality hardwood stores either in person or on line. Wood can be shipped, and often very good wood can be obtained that way.

Be sure that it is OK to cut wild wood before you do it. Ask the land owner. In some places anything growing on the sides of the road up to the fence lines is fine to cut, but not everywhere. Calling

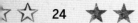

local tree services will sometimes get a whittler a lot of good wood for free. These people know wood, and they usually love to see some of it put to good use. Some wood that people cut up for firewood can be pretty good for whittlin', but try to get at it before the wood has lain around in the pile for a long time and become damaged.

Other materials for whittlin'

Some people cast blocks of plaster and whittle them.

Some whittle soap. Ivory soap mostly, and this can be a good material for younger kids to begin. Plastic or wooden knives can be used, though some whittlers use regular knives for this too. Some amazing things have been made out of soap.

Golf balls, and softballs. These are interesting materials, rubber, once the covers have been partially or totally removed.

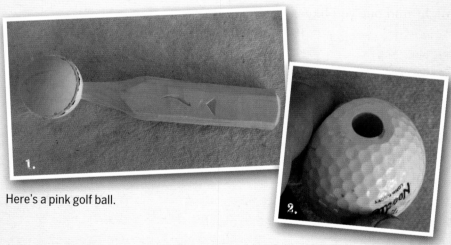

Here's a pink golf ball.

Drill a ⅜" hole first.

I usually drill a ⅜" hole first, and then whittle a handle out of wood, which is just jammed in the hole. That makes it easier to cut the cover using a hack saw, and then pry half of the cover off with a dull screwdriver.

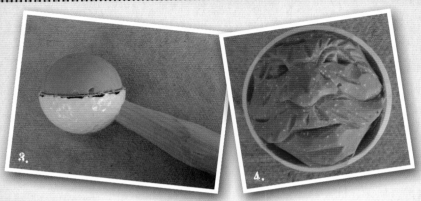

There, ready to whittle. Not all golf balls are of two piece construction but those that are, are easy to whittle. They come in a vast array of colors, and textures.

Here's a pink one with some spots.

And here is a white one. When the hole is drilled for the handle, the color of the center is instantly revealed.

They can be painted too, though I almost never do it.

I call these things golf ball trolls.

Every golfer should have one to prove that there is a little guy inside the ball making it do weird things, so it really isn't the golfer's fault!

Styrofoam. When I, because of my profession at the time, had to attend a lot of committee meetings, which were often pretty boring, I often resorted to whittlin' on my styrofoam coffee cup. I would whittle the surface of the cup into curly shavings that when finished made the cup look like it had a fur coat on! I was still able to follow the discussion, and kept my hands busy. Hey, it was better than strangling some of the people droning on with what they desperately wanted us all to believe was tremendously important.

CHAPTER FOUR

Techniques for Whittlin'

Well you've got that knife, and now it's good and sharp. It is time to cut something so this chapter is all about how to do that safely.

Understand that you will likely at some point cut yourself. This usually is not a very big deal compared to the kind of injuries that result from motor vehicle accidents or even falling off your bike. It is a pain however, and blood discolors the wood, so make every effort to avoid it.

The basic thing to remember is that the knife will slip. It is not a question of "if" but "when." Never cut in such a way that when the knife slips, any portion of you is in the way. Good and safe whittlin' is all about cutting wood and having fun. Take the time to figure out a way to make cuts on wood with no hazard to you.

When people get in a hurry they tend to let safety go out the window. Take it slow. Lots of little controlled cuts are far better than one or two big ones that are out of control. The word "control" is very important here. In order to make anything there has to be control. You need to be aware of and in control of your sharp edge at all times.

Reading this chapter first is good. Then get your knife and some straight grained, knot free sticks, and practice these techniques. Make lots of shavings. They make good fire starter if the wood is dry.

The first and most basic way to cut wood with a knife is pictured in **Photo 1**. Notice that the knife is grasped in the fist, with hardly any handle showing at the blade end. The handle is in contact with the palm and up against the web formed by the thumb and first finger. Do not hold the knife in your fingers. In my classes we call this a "girly grip," and it has no power. The pictured grip has power and if there is one thing a whittler needs, it is power.

I often see people grip a knife this way (**Photo 2**). This is not bad or dangerous, there just isn't the available power needed when a little force needs to be applied. I use it myself though for little cuts that don't need much force.

The best way to do the basic cut is to be sitting down at a comfortable height, with your forearms on the inside of your knees and the knife and work ahead of everything you don't want to cut (**Photo 3**).

Notice that the hand holding the stick is behind the cutting edge.

Your leg is **Not** a good workbench. Workbenches that bleed are never a good idea.

Stay well away from your legs with sharp items.

With the proper grip and position (**Photo 6**), wood can be efficiently and safely shaved off the stick. If the knife gets stuck in the cut, don't just yank on it, it could close on your finger. Just rock it from front to back a bit until it comes loose. Even better, just take small enough shavings, that getting stuck isn't an issue.

DO NOT DO THIS!!!

OR THIS!!

If you haven't done this before, it would be a good idea to turn several sticks into shavings just using this cut. In fact learning how to control this cut by making "feather sticks," on which the shavings remain on the stick is great whittlin' practice and produces the essential materials for starting good campfires.

This next cut looks dangerous, but is actually very safe, controllable, and powerful, if done correctly. Pay attention and practice this.

To start pinch the knife like this (**Photo 7**).

Then keeping the pinch, wrap the rest of the fingers around the knife handle (**Photo 8**).

Put the stick on the middle of your chest, with the non-knife hand out on the end as shown (**Photo 9**).

Do not change the grip on the knife.

Now, keeping the elbows down, with no change in the grip take some small shavings off the stick (**Photo 10**).

As this cut continues the knife hand will hit the body well before the blade can make contact (**Photo 11**). This is a good thing, and what makes this cut safe.

To cut right to the end of the stick, the knife hand is held steady against the body, and the stick is pulled out, away from the body by the holding hand. Notice the distance in **Photo 12** between the blade and the body. Again, a good thing!

Another view (**Photo 13**) of the finishing of that cut. Again, the blade is nowhere near the body.

This next cut is not for massive wood removal, but it is very precise and controllable.

Use one of your smaller blades (**Photo 14**) to get a feel for this. It will mostly be used with small blades anyway. By the way, the rule is to use the smallest blade that will do the job, not the biggest. For whittlin' bigger blades are awkward.

Hold the knife as pictured (**Photo 15**) with the thumb on the back of the blade.

With the stick in the fingers of the other hand, put the thumb of the non-knife hand on the back of the blade too, touching the knife thumb (**Photo 16**).

Put the blade onto the wood and push with the stick thumb only. No power at all should be coming from the knife hand. If when you are practicing this cut you go past the end of the stick and notice that there is "follow through", you are doing it wrong. The knife hand in this operation just puts the blade in position. All the power comes from the stick thumb. This enables the whittler to cut very precisely and, most importantly, to stop the cut exactly where desired.

In this picture (**Photo 17**) the stick thumb is on top of the knife thumb. Some people prefer to do it this way. Done properly and most safely, the thumbs are always touching.

I call this cut "the thumb push cut."

I call this next one, "the potato peeler cut."

Hold the knife as shown in **Photo 18** with the back of the blade nestled in the first finger. It is important to keep the fingers together, and have the back of the blade tucked in to the inside of the first knuckle.

The stick is held by the non-knife hand well behind the sharp edge (**Photo 19**).

The thumb of the knife hand is on the end of the stick out of line with the sharp edge, and the hand is squeezed to power the cut.

See how the edge misses the thumb (**Photo 20**). More good things!

21.

Another shot (**Photo 21**) of the thumb out of line of the blade.

People do cut themselves using this cut and I think I know why. They try to take too big of a bite. Then as they try to power the blade through the wood, the thumb gets in line with the blade and suddenly the wood gives way! Ouch! The solution is smaller cuts, less hurry. However, some people have trouble keeping their thumb out of the way with this cut, so using some kind of thumb guard is not a bad idea. A fairly thick wad of masking tape, duct tape or a wonderful rubberized product called "Vet Wrap" will make an effective thumb guard. Some whittlers just use the thumb of a glove.

Here is another powerful and safe cut that is useful even when using big blades. It is powerful enough to hog off a lot of wood when necessary, and yet is controllable enough for precision.

Start by holding the knife like this (**Photo 22**):

Notice that the edge is facing the hand and arm, and the handle is in the fingers.

Lay the thumb of the knife hand down on the side of the handle's end (**Photo 23**)—that shiny metal part is called the "bolster" on a knife like this. (Not all knives have them).

22.

23.

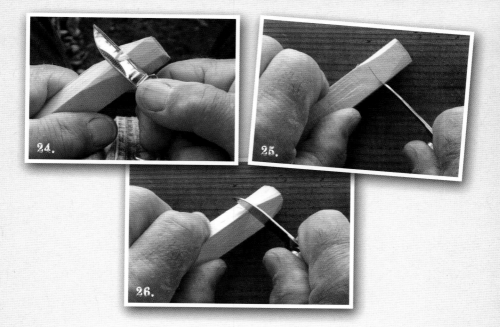

The stick is held in the other hand and brought up under the knife blade (**Photo 24**). The stick hand is behind the sharp edge.

The knuckles of both hands are against the body, and in a levering motion, those knuckles stay in contact with the body as both the blade and the stick are rotated outwards.

Sometimes the thumb of the stick hand is put on the back of the blade with this basic set up and the whole thing becomes a thumb push.

A fundamental concept in whittling is that of the "stop cut." This has to be understood if any decent work is going to be done. When a knife cuts wood, the wedging action of the blade splits the wood ahead of the cut. To prevent this split from ruining an element of the work that the whittler wants to keep, a cut is made down into the wood first like this (**Photo 25**). Using the point of the knife sometimes on a wide area, or using the sharp edge on a corner like this (**Photo 26**).

Please notice that these cuts are not being made down onto a leg, or a nice coffee table. They are onto an old board, that doesn't matter if it gets nicked up.

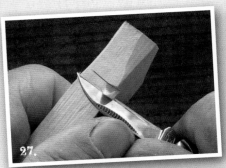

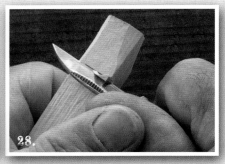

After the stop cut is made, a controlled cut, a thumb push in this case, is used to perform what is called a "clearing cut" (**Photo 27**). Actually several little clearing cuts (**Photo 28**) right up to the stop cut.

Putting the stick down on the old board and gently pushing down with the blade works too (**Photo 29**). Do not whittle up to a stop cut with the power cut, knife in fist, or the knife will go right on past the stop cut.

Practice making some nice clean notches using stop cuts and controlled clearing cuts.

In fact, it would be a good idea to have a bunch of sticks and just whittle them away using these instructions and practicing the various ways of whittlin'.

Especially practice the cuts that are the least familiar to you.

CLASSIC WHITTLING

CHAPTER FIVE

Toys

A flying helicopter toy

Here is a simple project that is one that I often use with beginning whittlers in my classes. It is not only fairly easy and fun to make, but when finished, it is fun to play with.

The kind of wood this project is made from is not important. Try to choose a piece that is straight grained and knot free. Split the wood with an axe or large knife until it is fairly close to the beginning size and then whittle it until you have a little board that looks like the one in the picture. Exact size is not important, but this one to start was 8" long by ⅞" wide by ¼" thick.

Make this as even as you can with nice sharp corners (**Photo 1**), and the rest will be much easier.

Find the center of the board using a ruler, and drill a hole right through the board (**Photo 2**). This hole should not angle off one way or the other but be as straight as possible. I used the awl on this Swiss army knife for this, but any drill will be fine. If using a drill, use one about ³⁄₁₆".

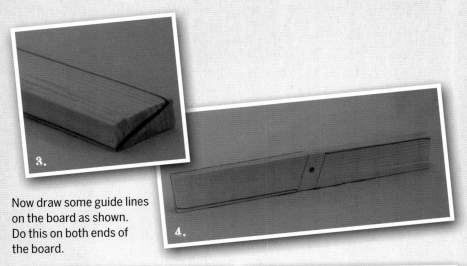

Now draw some guide lines on the board as shown. Do this on both ends of the board.

Carefully whittle the right hand corner off the board as shown, taking care to not cut off the guide lines, or to cut through them. Turn the piece end for end and do the same on the other end.

Flip the board over and repeat the action on the other side, always cutting off the right corner. Be careful to not cut through the edges.

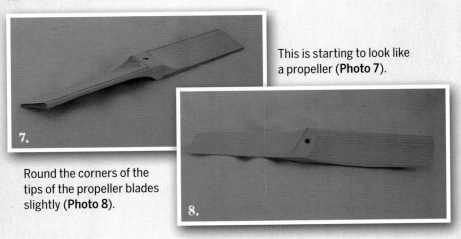

This is starting to look like a propeller (**Photo 7**).

Round the corners of the tips of the propeller blades slightly (**Photo 8**).

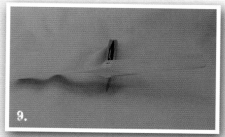

A propeller has to balance. Lay your knife on its back, edge up, line up the edge through the hole you drilled, and make a teeter totter out of it. You will quickly see if one end is heavier than the other.

Whittle a little wood off heavy end and check again until the propeller remains balanced.

Obtain a nice straight piece of wood that is about an 1" longer than the propeller.

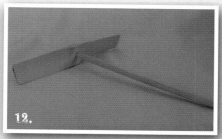

Whittle it until it is about the thickness of a regular pencil.

Taper one end of this stick so that it will fit snugly in the hole with a little drop of glue. If you use hot glue the project will be ready to fly right away.

To fly this toy, hold the propeller up, and put the stick on the heel of your left hand with the fingertips of your right hand (**Photo 13**).

Then push with your right hand while holding your hands together (**Photo 14**).

The stick and propeller will spin and fly up in the air. If it comes down and smacks your hands, you spun it the wrong way.

If you point the propeller at someone several yards away, and spin it at them they will be able to catch it and spin it back. If several people have these things, they can have helicopter wars, or contests to see which one can go the highest, or stay up the longest or...you will come up with all kinds of things.

If you want them to be colorful, use some felt markers and let your imagination just go wild!

These are great toys for whittlers to make for kids who don't know how to whittle—yet.

Making a real, working boomerang

What do you call a boomerang that doesn't come back? Answer at the end of the chapter.

These are great toys and a lot of fun to use. People are just amazed at how well they work, and when they find out that you made it—wow!

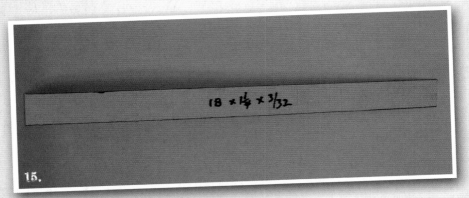

15.

Get two pieces of straight grained, knot free wood. I like to use spruce or white pine but lots of other kinds of wood will work as well. Look at the photo for the size. If you can saw the wood to that size, fine, but if you can't, just split the wood as close as possible to the size and then whittle it to the dimensions in the picture. It is important that you are very close to these measurements to start. It is especially important that with an 18" long boomerang stick that the piece be no wider than 1¼". A little narrower is OK, but wider doesn't work well.

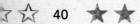

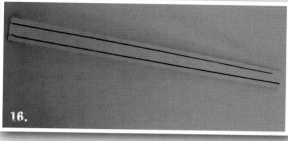

16.

17.

Draw some guidelines ¼" from the edges of the stick on one side (**Photo 16**). In my classes, I run a line along the bottom edge of the stick too as shown (**Photo 17**).

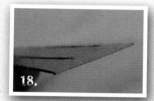

18.

Now using very careful cuts, thumb push cuts are good, bevel both edges as shown (**Photo 18**). Do not cut on the underside of the stick at all. It should remain perfectly flat. Use very controlled, small cuts to do this, so that if the grain "runs off" and kind of pulls your knife in, you can stop and cut in the other direction and not cut through the edge. If you do cut through the edge a little, keep going and try to do better. These boomerangs can be very crude and still work fine.

Once you have done both edges of the stick, round the corners slightly as shown, and then mark the middle of the stick, and make a mark 6" from each end.

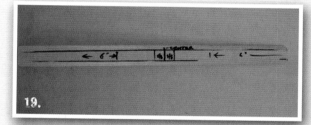

19.

Take a second stick, and do the same as you did on the first one, except better because you have some practice now, and mark the middle and 6" from the ends on it too.

20.

See if the sticks balance on the edge of your knife when lined up with that center line you drew. If they don't, fix them, by whittling a little wood off the heavy end.

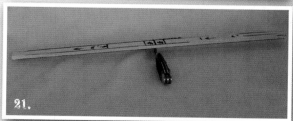

21.

22.

Put a little water on the marks that were made 6" from the ends. The water should go on both sticks, and on both ends and on both sides. Do not dip the sticks in water or hold them under the tap. Just wet your finger, and dab the water on. Let the water soak in for about 10 or 15 minutes. Then make a little bridge out of the two sticks between two 2x4's, as shown, with the flat sides of the sticks down.

23.

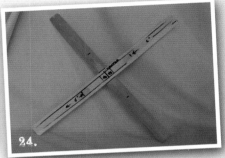

24.

Put something heavy like a pail of water on the sticks to make them bend. If they bend more than shown in the picture that is OK, but don't break them. Leave them for several hours, overnight is good. In the morning they will have a permanent bend.

Now glue the sticks together at right angles as shown, hot glue works well for this. I have even used tape or rubber bands so that I could collapse the boomerang later.

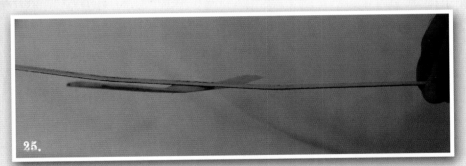

25.

See the bend.

 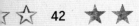

You want it to spin. If you throw it vertically with a spin, into the breeze, it will turn in the direction of the bend and come back. A little practice and you may even be able to catch it when it does return.

These boomerangs are light. The wind will affect them a lot. Don't fly them in a strong wind. Calm days are good. Flying them in a gymnasium is even better.

When you throw the boomerang, it must be close to vertical on release.

Be careful. If you run towards them while they are coming back you will get smacked in the face. They are however, a lot less dangerous than say a baseball if they hit you.

Stay well away from trees and buildings.

Try not to get them wet.

Felt pens can make them very colorful.

I once taught kids to make these boomerangs in Australia. You know, Australian kids don't automatically know how to make and throw boomerangs any more than Canadian kids know how to make igloos without being taught.

Another view. If you throw it like a Frisbee it will not come back.

Some of my students, after making their first few boomerangs, immediately started selling them and made themselves some money! Try to offer them for sale in a place where you can demonstrate them.

A boomerang that doesn't come back is called "a stick"!

Slip bark whistle. Music with a pocket knife?

Here is a classic whittlin' project. Whistles are such a standard product of the whittler's craft, that a lot of people, when they see someone with a knife and a stick immediately ask, "Making a whistle?" Sometimes, like now, the answer is "yes".

There was a time when all young boys and girls knew how to do this, back in the day when a man or boy was not dressed without a knife in his pocket. Lots of girls and women carried pocket knives too. No one is born with the ability to do these things though, so this segment is here to show you how.

Before you even start, there are a few things to keep in mind. The first is that this can only be done when the sap is actively flowing in the tree. In the northern parts of North America, this means spring. These demonstration pictures were done in February in southern California, but in Idaho, it will be April or May before this is possible.

Lots of different kinds of trees/bushes will work for this. Traditionally, willow has been used, and these whistles are often called "willow whistles" for that reason. The photos here are showing a piece of willow, but actually, I prefer to use Douglas maple (Oregon maple). Alder, aspen, service berry (Saskatoon berry) and even cedar can be used, but it is probably easier to use willow. There are dozens of different kinds of willow.

You need to be aware that you likely will have to make several attempts at this before you "get it." There are a lot of little details in this seemingly simple project, where things can go wrong. Don't give up! Millions of children have learned to do this. You can learn it too.

Please read these instructions all the way through and understand them before you begin.

When you do this, always work off the top of the branch (**Photo 28**). That is because branches taper from bottom to top. If you try to take a small tube of bark off of a larger piece of wood the bark will split. Taking a larger piece of bark off of a smaller piece of wood works. The branch will show you, which is the top. The twigs and buds on the branch point up. The branch must be freshly cut from a live bush or tree. Even after only a few hours, the wood is too dry to work. Also, all this work needs to be done in one session. If you lay it aside for a few hours and then come back, you will have problems.

Cut a piece of branch that is free of twigs and large buds (**Photo 29**). At the top end cut it to and angle as shown. There must be no tears or splits anywhere in the bark. If there are, it will be necessary to start again.

Carefully whittle a little flat on the end of the angled cut (**Photo 30**). Cut towards the center of the stick while doing this. If you cut from the center out, the bark will tear and you will need to cut back further beyond the torn part.

Make sure your knife is really sharp for this. It should be super sharp all the time anyway.

Then make a cut all the way around the stick, through the bark and into the wood. Try to make this a neat one line cut as shown.

Now close your knife and hold it like this (**Photo 31**).

Put the whistle stick down on a firm surface, or even your leg. It's OK to tap on your leg with a closed knife. Now tap the bark all over on the part that you will be removing. The tapping should be hard enough to bruise the bark but not break it. This is hard to explain. Experience will teach you. Sometimes rubbing the bark firmly with another stick that has had the bark peeled off will help loosen the bark too.

The bark must be tapped/rubbed all over. Tapping just here and there will not do it.

After the tapping and rubbing all over, grasp the bark that is to be removed firmly in one hand and the other part of the stick in the other hand, give it a twist. If it is the right time of year and you have done everything right up to this point, the bark will release with a little "pop".

If you can slide the tube of bark off the end with your thumb like this, with no splits, celebrate! If you can do this, the rest becomes possible. Do not attempt to forge ahead if there are splits in the bark, because the whistle has no hope of working if there are, and there will be no way of knowing if you have done the rest correctly.

Take a few moments to congratulate yourself and marvel at the wonderful thing that you have accomplished (**Photo 35**).

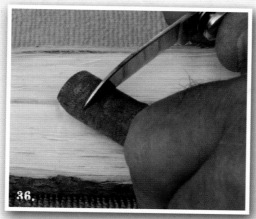

Now back to work. Put the bark back on the stick exactly in the position it was before it was removed. Put the whistle blank on something firm. A log, board, or table is good.

Anyway once you have found a good, safe and firm surface, cut down through the bark and slightly into the wood as shown.

Then holding the bark in position and using a thumb push cut, cut up towards the first cut and take out a little wedge of bark and wood.

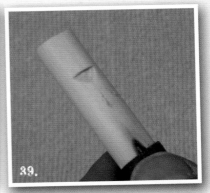

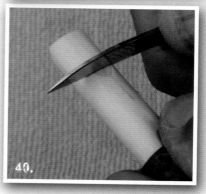

Do a few tiny cuts until the result is like this (**Photo 38**). Do not make the notch bigger than this.

Slip the bark off without crushing it and put it in a safe place. There should be a little notch in the wood which will guide you in making the next cuts (**Photo 39**).

Right on the little cut that was made right through the bark and into the wood while cutting on the safe firm surface, cut deeper (**Photo 40**).

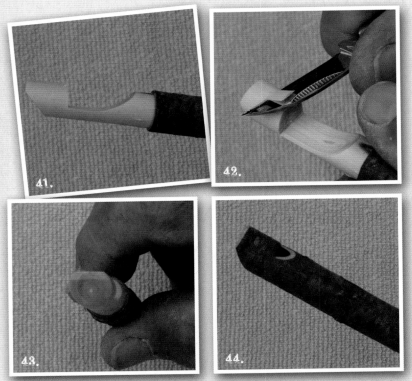

Use thumb push cuts only! This is important. If you use other cuts you will almost certainly cut off part of the mouthpiece end, called the fipple. If this happens you will have to start completely over with a new branch. I have seen this done many times, trust me and do it right.

Whittle it down at least this much (**Photo 41**). This is the sound chamber. The bigger this is the deeper the tone of the whistle. Beginners often make the sound chamber too small and the whistle won't work. Well, it may actually be working, but the sound is so high only dogs can hear it, and they won't tell you. Take your time and do it right.

Now we come to a place where lots of new whistle makers have messed up and had to start all over again. Carefully whittle a *little* flat spot on the top of the mouthpiece end (**Photo 42**). Just a little. This is easy to make bigger if necessary, but the whole thing will have to be started over if it is made too big, so only cut a little off. It does need to be even and flat, so that when the bark is put back on, and the whistle is blown, air can get into the sound chamber.

Here is another view of the flat spot on the fipple (**Photo 43**).

Put the bark back on and blow (**Photo 44**). Don't cover the sound hole with your lips. If you get a nice clear whistle—great!

If not, don't give up. Maybe the little flat spot just needs to be a tiny bit larger, try that first. Then go back over all the steps and see if there is a place where things need to be improved and try again.

The old expression, "clean as a whistle", does not actually refer to sanitation, though, we all want our whistles to be germ free. What it actually means is that the cuts need to be precise and sharp with no snaggy bits hanging on. Cuts need to be clean, or it will be difficult to make a working whistle.

The amazing and mysterious Yipstick

When people see you working this toy, they will really believe that you are a magician.

What does it do? It amazes and mystifies! With the results of your whittlin' and some practice, you can totally mystify, and amaze too, almost everyone who sees this work.

This is a pretty simple project, yet one that demands some care in making and some practice in the using for the finished product to actually do a good job of amazing and mystifying.

As with all of the projects in this book, it is important to read through and understand the instructions before coming back to the beginning and starting in on the actual work. Don't just look at the photos. It will make a difference in how well this will work.

Sticks about the size of those in **Photo 45** are excellent yipstick material. Slightly larger or smaller in diameter will work too.

Choose one stick and a good sharp knife (**Photo 46**), and let's get to work.

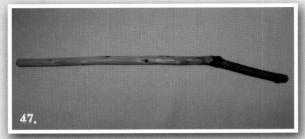
47.

48.

Whittle off the knots, and take the bark off the long straight part. It is OK to take the bark off the handle too, but I think leaving it on adds to the woodsy/whittled nature of this thing. Make the stick as smooth as possible.

Whittle two flat spots that almost come together at a ridge along the entire top edge of the peeled part of the stick.

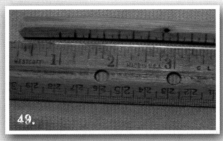
49.

50.

Get a ruler and pencil out, and along that ridge, make a mark every ⅛". Make every second one longer, so that there is ¼" between the long lines.

Put the stick on a safe surface and make a stop cut straight down on the ridge at every one of the long lines. Do not make stop cuts on the short lines.

51.

52.

Using thumb push cuts; and it is really important that you use this cut on this project, cut down from the short lines, the ones between the stop cuts, to the stop cuts. Then turn the stick around and come at that same stop cut from the other way, and repeat this all along the ridge.

Do not cut toward your hand like this. Trust me. I have bled plenty, and I know how it works.

The idea is to make a series of even points and notches all along the ridge of the stick.

Be very careful to not break or cut off any of the points. The little lines should be visible on every point when it is done. Take your time, make little cuts and do not twist the knife or pry at all, because your yipstick will not work well with broken off points.

Another stick will be used to make a sort of "propeller." **Photo 54** shows that this other stick is a little thinner than the main stick and there is a little notch cut about 2" from its end, where after a little work it will be cut off, but for now the rest of the stick will provide a handle to make the work easier to hold.

Flatten the center on one side, flip it over and flatten the other side, thinning it in the middle and then cut the propeller off (**Photo 55**).

Somewhere close to the middle drill a little hole through the propeller (**Photo 56**). The hole making blade on this knife is perfect for this, but a regular drill can be used too. If a campfire is near, and a pair of pliers and a pair of gloves are available, the nail that will be needed in the next step can be heated in the campfire and the hole can be burned through.

It is very important to not split the propeller in making the hole. If doing it the way the photo shows, take it easy and drill from both sides. If it does split, make a new one. It's just a stick!

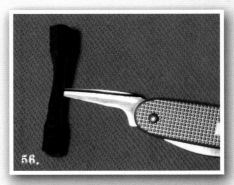

A nail about this size (**Photo 57**) is needed.

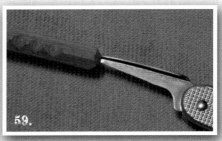

Put the nail through the hole and give it a few spins. The propeller should fit loosely over the nail. Do not attempt to balance the propeller. It will actually work better if it is out of balance a bit. It should not be radically out of balance though.

Start a little hole in the end of the notched stick. This could also be done by burning. Take extreme care not to split the stick. If an electric drill is available, a drill just a tiny bit smaller than the nail, or another nail with the head cut off, can be used as a drill to start the hole.

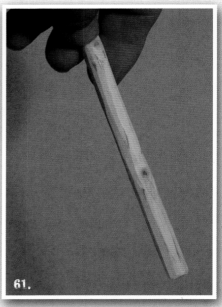

Put the propeller on the nail and then tap the nail in the end of the stick just enough that it is tight, but not enough to split the stick.

There should be a lot of excess space between the end of the stick and the head of the nail as shown.

Peel another stick 4 or 5" long and about the same thickness as the notched stick. The thickness really doesn't matter much. Make it bark free and smooth.

Now it is important to really pay attention and practice what the next few sentences say and the next couple of photos show.

Hold the notched stick in one hand by the handle, and the smooth stick just like the right hand is doing in **Photo 62**. Notice that the pointer finger is touching the notched stick though not the notches, on its left side.

Rub the little stick back and forth on the notches, while keeping the pointer finger touching the left side of the notched stick. While that pointer finger is touching the stick do not allow the thumb or any other fingers to touch the notched stick. The propeller will start to spin and if you rub faster it will spin faster.

If it does not spin, study the photo and try again, making sure that only the rubbing stick and the pointer finger are touching the notched stick while the rubbing takes place.

Now while continuing to rub, slide the rubbing stick over just a bit so that the pointer finger is not touching the notched stick at all, but the thumb tip is and keep rubbing.

See how the thumb is now touching (**Photo 63**).

The propeller will stop and reverse its direction when the other side is touched. I don't know why it does this but it does. Magic is sometimes hard to explain.

So, after you have got this switching the contact from the finger to the thumb practiced up, and you can do this while rubbing pretty briskly, you can come up with a story about how you have made this little contraption, and in the process trained the propeller to respond to a voice command. Come up with a magic word. I use the word "yip." Every time I say the word, I tend to say it with a great deal of emphasis. This usually makes everyone jump a bit. I move my hand just enough to change whether it is my finger or my thumb that is in contact with the yipstick, and the propeller reverses. When others say the word, I don't change so it doesn't work. The propeller only listens to me!

It is important to practice this in private so that the hand is moving quite quickly and observers can't see the little shift. Don't point the propeller directly at any observers either, because they could see what you are doing that way.

This will totally baffle most people. They might think they know how you do it and will want to try. Let them. Most will be frustrated, and you can have a lot of fun with this.

Of course, you can use any magic word that you want. Some people use the word "hooey" so for them it is a hooey stick.

Others say "Gee" to make the propeller go right, and "Haw" to make it go left. These people call their sticks "Gee Haw Wammydiddles."

Don't tell how you do it unless they buy the stick from you! Charge whatever you want, and the market will bear, and then take them off in private to explain and let them practice. This will drive other onlookers up the wall! Who knows, you might become a successful yipstick maker. I have seen them for sale, and have sold quite a few myself.

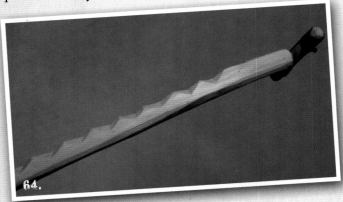

Here is one with bigger notches. They work too, but I have found that smaller notches work better for beginners.

If this doesn't work for you at first don't give up. You will get it.

CHAPTER SIX
Whittlin' Treen

Amazingly, the "wand" can be used to make practical things. Treen are utensils like forks, spoons and ladles that are usually whittled out of green wood and are meant to be used. Green wood is wood that has not been allowed to dry. The fact that the results of your whittlin' can actually be used makes this kind of work extra special.

The easiest piece of treen, and one that many people who wouldn't think of themselves as whittlers have made, or tried to make, is a twig fork for roasting a wiener or a marshmallow. The same basic fork can be made a lot smaller for eating things that need to be poked in order to be picked up, like say, sardines or small pieces of cheese.

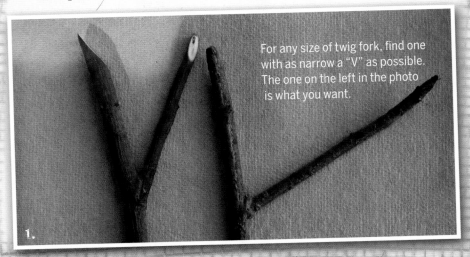

For any size of twig fork, find one with as narrow a "V" as possible. The one on the left in the photo is what you want.

1.

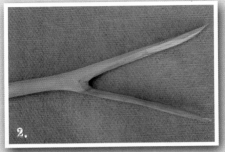

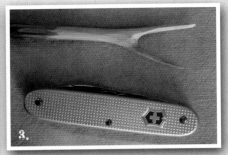

Carefully peel off all of the bark, so that none gets on your food or flavors it in ways you don't want. Thin down the wood where it seems necessary, and sharpen the tips. Of course the stick needs to be cut to a length that will enable you to cook with it without cooking yourself.

For forks used to eat off of a plate, everything just needs to be scaled down.

Making a wooden spatula and a serving fork

For this project a sapling or branch that is about 2" to 3" in diameter is needed. Get one that is as straight and with as few little branches as possible. Try to get a piece of willow, aspen, alder, tulip poplar or birch. Other kinds of wood will work too, but try to avoid softwoods like pine or cedar.

This little log needs to be split in half to start. If there is already a split in the log, start with that.

If there is a tiny crack like this on the log, work with it too.

Using hand pressure only, make a cut into the end of the log, following any crack that is already there.

This is all that is needed.

Next whittle a little wedge like the one in the photo from any available scrap of wood...

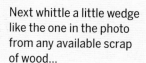

...and tap the wedge into the little cut that was made with the knife. It is absolutely amazing, how big of a log can be split using just some whittled wooden wedges.

Just add more wedges as necessary to complete the split.

Use your knife and whittle off the edges. One edge has been done here.

There, a couple of nice pieces for our purpose.

Notice that none of the very center of the log, the pith, is left on this blank. Making sure that this is the case helps avoid having the finished piece split as it dries out.

It is a good idea to not do this green woodwork in the hot sun. Hot sun on wet wood is not a good combination. Get in the shade, and do not leave a semi finished project in the sun. It is better, if the work has to be left a while, to put it in a plastic bag. If it has to be left for several days, it is good to put it in the plastic bag and then put it in the freezer. In the freezer, it will be fine for a very long time.

With this project the centermost part of the log will become the back side of the spatula or fork, but that orientation is not absolutely necessary. Either way will work fine.

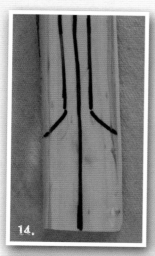

14.

Now rough sketch the over all shape of the carving on the blank, top (**Photo 14**) and side view (**Photo 15**). Actually, I find it best to whittle the top view shape first, and then sketch the side view.

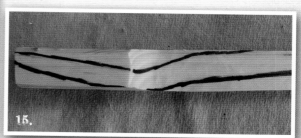

15.

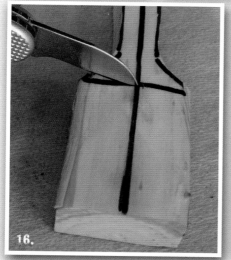

16.

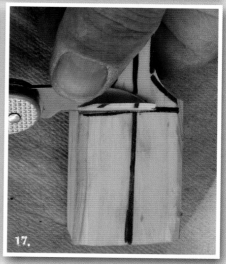

17.

Then whittle it. Here a stop cut is made where the most dished part of the top of the spatula will be formed.

Then using controlled cuts work towards that stop cut, deepening it as necessary (**Photo 17**) until the required depth has been reached. (**Photo 18**).

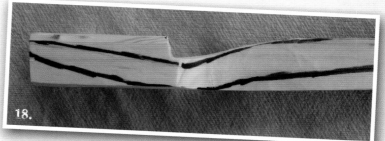

18.

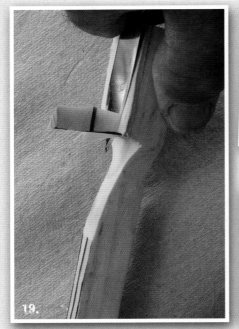

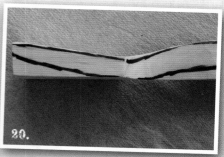

This is where this is all heading.

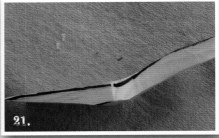

Then work from the other side of the stop cut with whatever safe cutting will do the job. Here, a cross grain potato peeler kind of cut is being used. Notice that the thumb is not in line with the blade.

Then shape the under side, which will be a little easier.

Refine and even up the overall shape as much as you want.

Here are some little details that can make a real difference in producing a spatula that is light, lively in the hand and still good and strong. Notice how the edges of the blade and handle are whittled thin for lightness, but the center is left thicker for strength. Both sides would be done of course.

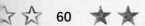

Everything needs to be evened up (**Photo 24**), smoothed, rounded, and in the case of the front edge, sharpened (**Photo 25**), to make a functional kitchen utensil (**Photo 26**).

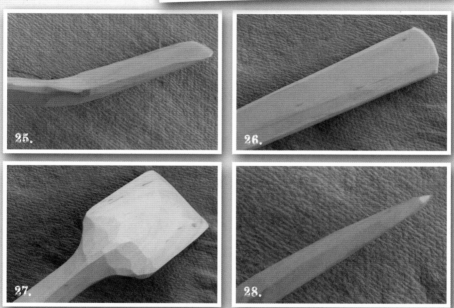

Here are a few views that will help in achieving this. (**Photos 27 & 28**)

Spatulas like this are very useful in the kitchen, and can be used immediately, or allowed to dry, out of the sun. In very dry areas it might be a good idea to dry it inside a paper bag to slow the drying a bit. Once dry it can be sanded, and rubbed with mineral oil, or it can even be boiled in beeswax. However, do not heat beeswax directly over an element or flame indoors. It is better to do this on a camp stove out doors to lessen the risk of fire.

Serving or salad fork

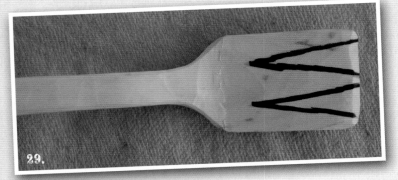

To make a large serving or salad fork, just make a spatula as above and turn it into a fork.

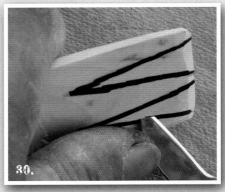

Sketch the tines on and whittle away, always using safe, controlled cuts.

This is the **wrong** way. **Do not do this**. There is danger to the whittler with a cut like this, and a great risk of destroying the project besides.

Here is a safe way of doing this; notice the thumb is not in line with the blade.

If you have a good, sharp saw, it can help speed up the process. A band saw would be even better, and a coping saw could be used too. This handy folding Silky Saw is great to have along when the well equipped wood shop is far away.

Just make everything look "forky", and its done!

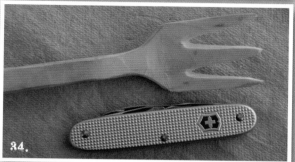

Another fork

I often make myself a quick little fork like this when I'm out hiking.

A small piece of wood is usually easy to find, and clean up. Again, don't leave any of the center of the branch in the blank.

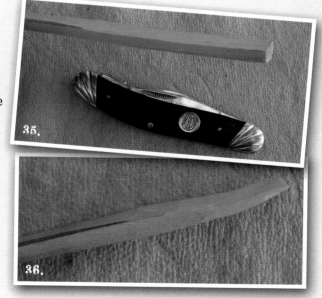

Give the fork end a little shape like this.

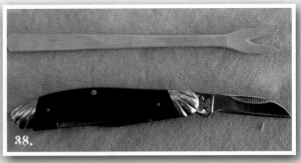

Sketch in a couple of tines (**Photo 37**), and whittle it out (**Photo 38**). When the meal is over, this can be totally cleaned up by the camp fire.

Spoon

A classic project for whittlers, and treen whittlers especially, is a spoon.

Here is how to make one if you just have a minimum of tools.

Dimensions and species used are in the photo, but size is obviously quite variable. The wood used could be maple, alder, aspen, tulip poplar, and others. Avoid coniferous woods for this because the flavors of the resins in those woods get transferred to the food.

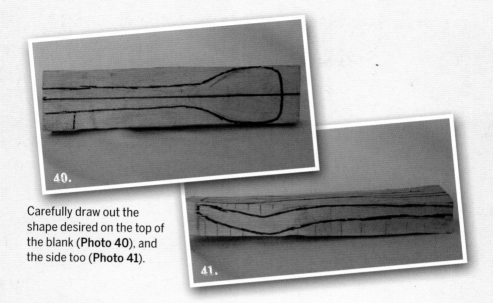

40.

41.

Carefully draw out the shape desired on the top of the blank (**Photo 40**), and the side too (**Photo 41**).

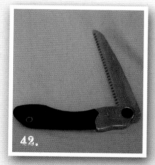

42.

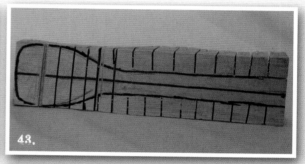

43.

The Silky Saw will be used for the next part, though other saws will work fine too.

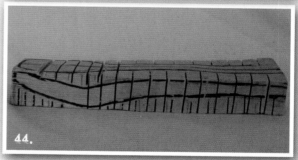

44.

Cut almost down to the sketched lines as shown, from the sides (Photo 43) and top and bottom (Photo 44).

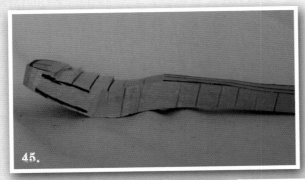

45.

Using a knife or even a sharp and carefully used hatchet, split off the little blocks of waste wood.

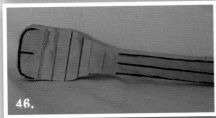

46.

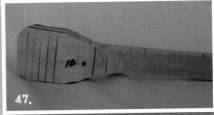

47.

It is still rather rough in these photos (**46** & **47**), but with the knife, it can all be smoothed out and evened up (**Photo 48**).

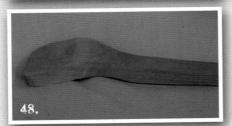

48.

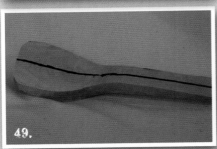

49.

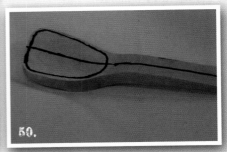

50.

It is very important to draw a center line on the spoon, if you want to carve one that is symmetrical. If you want a free form spoon that is not symmetrical, well then the center line isn't so important. This one is being made symmetrically.

Sketch in the shape of the bowl, leaving about ⅛" around the sides and front.

Notice that the front edge of the bowl is very shallow (**Photo 52**). If it is made deeper at the front edge, there will be a tendency for that part to chip out both while it is being made, and later in use.

The deepest part of the spoon is near the handle, but even that is not all that deep in a spoon. Spoons are for stirring and maybe tasting and serving smaller portions. Deeper spoons are properly called ladles, and are for serving bigger amounts of soups and stews. If you want to make a ladle, adjust the dimensions accordingly, but try to maintain the shallow front end for strength.

It is possible to hollow out the bowl part with just a knife, and I have done it many times, but using the proper tools does a much better job and is a lot easier.

One way of doing this is to use what is called a bent knife. These are sometimes called "Crooked Knives" or "Hook Knives".

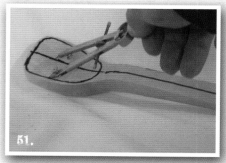

The use of a compass or dividers is helpful in getting everything even.

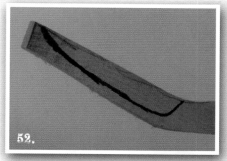

This sketch is a kind of "X-ray vision" look at what the inside of the bowl will be shaped like.

The hollowing is the hard part.

If you use one of these, make sure it is really sharp and carve across the grain as much as possible, with lots of small cuts.

One kind of laborious way of making the bowl of a spoon, that I have not illustrated, is to get a hot coal from a fire onto the blank and blowing on it. The coal will burn down a bit, and the charring can be scraped away, and the process repeated. This takes time, but works quite well.

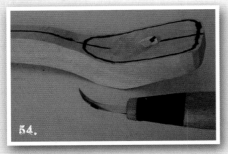

54.

I use a bent knife for this work on occasion, and it works fairly well. Some spoon makers prefer them.

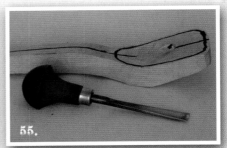

55.

Normally, I prefer to use a gouge.

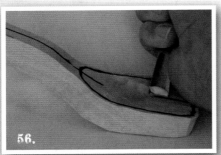

56.

I grip the gouge as shown, with just a little bit of the sharp end protruding past my hand. Then I put the heel of the tool holding hand on the work piece and just rotate my wrist to make the cut as shown. If just a little bit of the tool protrudes past my hand and the heel of the hand is kept in contact with the work, this is a very safe way to cut.

Little cuts only! Do not strain. Straining leads to slips. We don't want those!

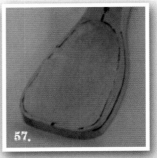

57.

Finish up as much of the hollowing as possible at this point.

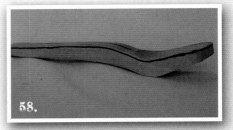

58.

Then draw a guide line about ⅛" below the top edge of the entire spoon.

59.

60.

Shave down the bowl area as shown, being careful to work with or across the grain and not against it to prevent splitting off parts that you want to keep. Without cutting through the side guide lines, thin down the bowl area of the spoon quite a lot leaving the junction of the bowl and handle area fairly thick.

Use your fingers to gauge the thickness as you go. Don't cut through!

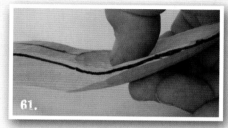

61.

Thicker here.

Again, a centerline can be useful.

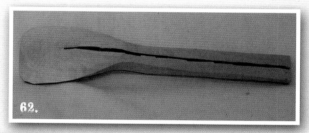

62.

63.

Notice how one side has been carved almost down to the finished dimension.

64.

Study the next couple of pictures to see how the handle/bowl junction should be shaped for lightness and strength.

This area should take on a kind of triangular shape.

That shape is pretty obvious in this photo.

The handle itself can be thinned down.

Here is another view of that triangular handle/bowl junction.

Now the edge can be bevelled or rounded as desired and the spoon is ready to go.

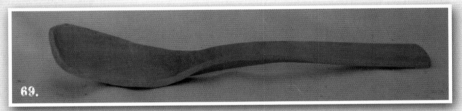

I tend to make my spoons with wide flat handles, to make them easier to grasp without twisting, and to give more area for decoration. All kinds of handle configurations are possible of course.

Spoons like this are very useable just the way they are, or they can be sanded after drying. Whether sanded or not, they can be oiled with mineral oil, walnut oil or flaxseed oil (food grade) or even boiled in beeswax. I have never done it, but some spoon makers boil their spoons in milk, and say that this produces a good finish.

If you do a few spoons and start getting good at it, you may find that a demand for this product will be created, because a spoon like this really has no equal. Plastic and even wooden spoons can be purchased at the supermarket, but they are not even close to as good as a hand whittled one that is done right.

CHAPTER SEVEN

Intricate Whittlin'

As with other forms of magic, the comment "How did you do that?" is often brought forth by applying your handy folding "magic wand" in the following ways.

The impossible arrow

This little project is actually a lot easier than it looks. People are totally fascinated by the result though, and you can sell the finished products.

Sometimes this is done using a glass bottle with a hole drilled through it to insert the arrow, but that involves, well, drilling a hole through a bottle, and that is a lot harder than the actual trick of getting a wooden arrow through a hole that is too small for it. Drilling through a bottle isn't impossible of course, but involves tools that most whittlers won't have. Another good, and easy to drill item, is a golf ball or a baseball.

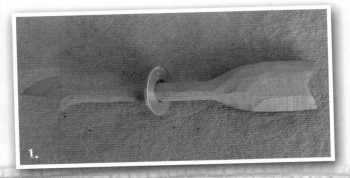

1.

The photos show a washer and a golf ball, but you could obviously let your imagination run wild here.

Whatever subject you decide to go through, you need to first get wood for the arrow. I have done this trick using either white pine or basswood, but I am sure that other kinds of wood could be used too. Don't hesitate to experiment.

Make a little board out of knot free wood that is a little thinner than the hole that it will need to go through, and with the growth rings going in the direction of the black lines in the photo. I have done this with the rings going the other way too, but it seems to work a little better this way, at least with the kinds of wood that I have used.

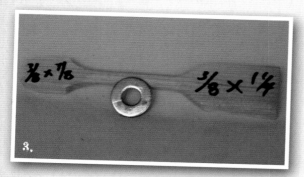

Then rough whittle the arrow to the dimensions shown on the photo. Pictured is a ⅜" washer. Obviously, if you want this project to be bigger or smaller, the dimensions will need to be adjusted.

Do not finish the arrow any more than shown in the photo at this point.

The arrowhead end of the blank needs to be soaked in water for at least a day.

Once the wood is well soaked, put it in a vise.

6.

Squeeze the arrow head end down until it is smaller than the arrow shaft. Leave it there overnight.

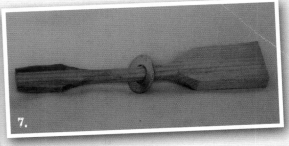

7.

When the vise is loosened, you will be able to put the arrowhead through the washer. You may have to whittle the corners of the arrowhead a little to make that happen. Then put the arrowhead back in the water, and after a while it will pop out to its original width.

At this point, you can whittle the arrowhead and feathers as much as you want, but be sure to leave them wide enough to totally mystify anyone who looks at it.

I have sold these things using washers and golf balls and I am sure that putting them through, bottles, baseballs and what have you would attract a lot

8.

of interest and even some dollars.

It is better if you don't tell everyone how this is done. Or even anyone! Let's just keep this a whittler's secret.

Chain

At the age of 10 or 11 I had already used my knife to make little boats, slingshots and other stuff, but when I saw a picture of a wooden chain and then later actually made one—well—I was infected! I caught the whittlin' bug bad and have had it ever since.

I came up with a system of making chains and made a lot of them, but later found that I had been doing it the hard way. The way I am about to describe is not that way. This way is much better than my old method.

If this is your first chain, I would suggest getting a piece of basswood if you can. Aspen would be good too, or tulip poplar. Avoid woods that split easily.

I know what I am about to say will be ignored by many, but please read through all of the steps and try to understand them before starting to cut. It really will make this easier to do.

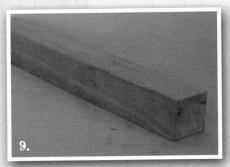

Chains can be any size you like. I have even seen some made out of a wooden match. However, to start use a 1"x1" x10" piece of wood, without knots.

Draw some guide lines as illustrated. Whittlers remember; your pencil is your friend.

Following the lines, carefully whittle out the grooves as shown. Do not cut deeper than the bottom of that groove. Do this as far along the stick as you want to make the chain.

Now you need to decide how long each of your chain links will be, and using a little stick with that length marked on it, lay out the links on your work piece as shown. At this point it is OK to whittle off the wood marked with an "X" in the picture.

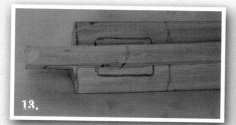

Then sketch in the inside of the links.

I did them first with a pencil, which should be sufficient, but in the next pictures have used a felt pen so that you can see the marks better.

Make stop cuts on the inside ends of the link as shown.

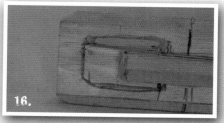

Then carefully, with controlled, tiny cuts remove the wood between the stop cuts.

Do this, working from all four sides until it looks like this.

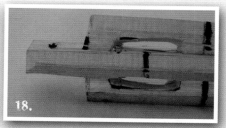

Repeat on the next link.

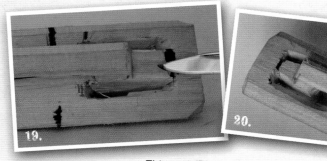

This part (**Photo 19**) was left to support the whole structure while you work on the hard part, which is, carefully working from all sides, to separate the first two links (**Photo 20**).

21.

22.

Now take out that little bit that was left for strength (**Photo 21**), and whittle that first link free (**Photo 22**).

23.

24.

You have freed up your first link! Time for a little celebration!

If you haven't already marked the next link, use your measuring stick to do so,

25.

26.

and just repeat the process that was used on the first link.

You can clean up the links as you go or rough them all out and clean them up later.

27.

Here are a few chains that I have made.

28.

This one is from the "doing it the hard way" days, when I further complicated things by using branches, or saplings with the pith in the center as you can see. This one is made from a hard wood too—ash or oak. I made this about 1972.

29.

Interlinked hearts

Here's a snazzy little gift for Valentine's Day.

Actually, whittlin' interlocked hearts is just like making a chain of two links with each link in the shape of a heart. The first step is to make your blank square, 2"x2"x10" should be good, though you could make it any size. This example is made of basswood, but this is a great project for using other kinds of wood with more interesting grain. It is a good idea to have done a few chains before doing this one though, especially if you are going to use harder wood.

30.

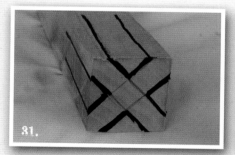

31.

Mark out the "X" from corner to corner on the blank.

32.

Carefully whittle out the inside corners, remembering to not cut deeper than the point of the grooves.

Draw out the hearts, as shown (**Photos 33 & 34**) and rough whittle them partially to shape (**Photo 35**).

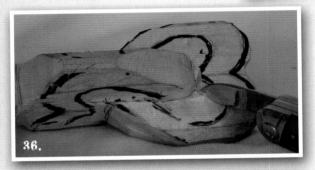

Put stop cuts in place to prevent splitting the heart at both ends of what will become your clearing cuts (**Photos 36 & 37**).

Then start clearing out the wood from the inside of the end heart, alongside the second heart.

Do a little on one side (**Photo 39**), and then repeat the stop cuts and the clearing on the other side, back and forth, until you get this result (**Photo 40**).

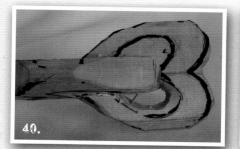

Move on to the other side and do it the same way (**Photo 41**).

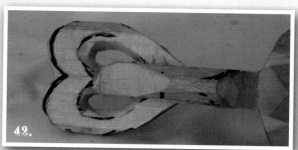

Leave that little bit on the center inside of the first heart and the center outside of the second heart. It will strengthen the whole whittlin' while you are working on the inside of the hearts. Notice that in the photos, the second heart has not been cut free of the rest of the stick. That stick is helpful as a handle to make the whole thing a lot easier to hang on to.

Move on to the second heart and repeat what was done to the first one.

Now begin separating the hearts at the inner intersection. Use careful, controlled cuts, do not pry! Do a little on one corner, then a little on another, working your way around all four inner corners until you have gone right through.

Once that has all been done, whittle out that little bit at the outside end of each heart, here (**Photo 45**), and here (**Photo 46**), making sure that everything is free here too **Photos 47** & **48**).

Be careful to not damage the heart shape while doing all of this.

There! The one piece is now two.

  80 ★ ★

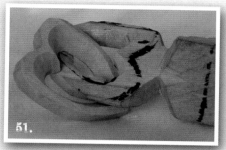

51.

I like to clean up the hearts and give them whatever shape I want while the second heart is still attached to the handle.

52.

Once that is done the second heart can be whittled off the handle, and finished up.

There, romantic symbolism and folk art. What a combination!

You could of course make a whole chain of hearts. I'm not quite sure about the symbolism of many hearts entwined though.

Ball in cage

Here is another one of those whittler's "tricks" that amazes people but is actually rather easy to do. Easier than a chain, I think.

Start out with a square stick. For your first effort, I would suggest about 1"x1" x 10". It is always best to have enough stick to hold on to.

I would use basswood, white pine, or aspen. Birch, walnut, or even mahogany would be good too. For the first time use softer woods. It will make it a lot easier if the wood is knot free.

These are often done on the end or in the middle of a chain carving.

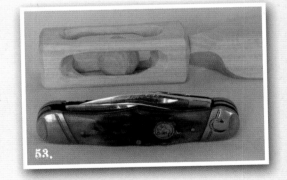

53.

I have two daughters. When each of them got married, I whittled a ball in cage and chain and presented it to my sons-in-law at the respective receptions. You can figure out the symbolism.

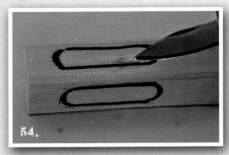

Draw some guide lines as shown on the stick. The corners of the stick will become the "posts" of the cage.

With a sharp, pointed blade, and working from all four sides, whittle a hole at both ends of the cage. You could use a drill for this, but that might be considered cheating.

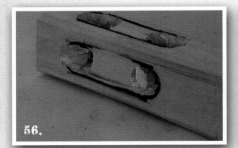

The holes become stop cuts to prevent splitting when you carefully whittle diagonal slits as shown.

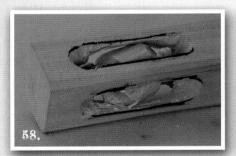

Take your time. This will involve working in from eight surfaces until the chunk of wood inside the cage becomes loose.

Then it is just a matter of whittling the chunk round, and cleaning up the ends and posts of the cage.

A more complicated ball in cage

60.

61.

62.

Take a 6" piece of straight grained, knot free wood that you like, and make it round (**Photo 61**), and about 1½" in diameter. This cage will have three bars, so mark the center of the bars on the end of the wood (**Photo 62**).

63.

64.

Use some strips of paper and pins to lay out the spiral bars. Make them as even as you can. Use your pencil and sketch until you are happy with the results.

I have gone over the pencil lines here with a fine tipped felt pen to make the lines easier to see.

65.

66.

Whittle holes at each end. Remember there are only three posts, so you will not go straight through like you did on the simple cage. Do this at only one end of the cage for now.

Carefully make stop cuts just outside of the lines drawn to depict the posts of the cage.

Clear out some of the wood towards the stop cuts. Thumb push cuts are good for this.

Then clear out the "hump" in between the posts, and start undercutting the posts, a little at a time on all sides.

Remember not to pry, and to keep your knife razor sharp.

Keep working carefully and patiently until your knife will fit like this all the way down each of the posts.

Now start making a ball out of the end of the inner wood where the holes were whittled.

When that first ball comes free, there should be plenty of wood left to make another one.

Of course you could use a longer piece of wood and have several balls however, you will need to keep in mind that the posts will be weaker and flex more as they get longer. You might want to use a stronger piece of wood if you are going to make it longer than this one.

74.

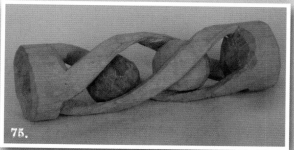

75.

Once the balls are done it is time to clean up the rest of the piece.

There!
This could be whittled as the end or middle of a chain.

Ring on a dumbbell

This whittlin' can be done out of just about any scrap of wood that doesn't have cracks in it. A sapling or a branch from a tree would work too. You could even leave some bark on the ends of the dumbbell.

This could be done on the end of a hiking stick, or maybe with more than one ring to make a baby's rattle.

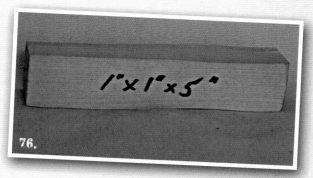

1"x 1"x 5"

76.

This stick will work fine in these dimensions, as a first try.

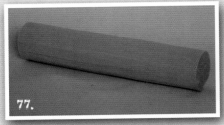

77.

Whittle the stick round first. If it is
a branch or a sapling, you can skip
the rounding.

78.

Mark the position of the ring.

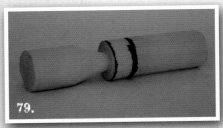

79.

Using stop cuts and careful, controlled
clearing cuts, narrow the center of the
dumbbell, leaving the ring.

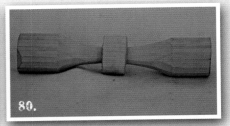

80.

Take your time and make this as even and
as "clean" (not ragged), as you can.

81.

Start gently undercutting the ring.
Do not pry! Work from both sides
being careful not to thin the handle
of the dumbbell too much.

82.

Once you get through, clean
everything up and shape the ends
as desired. The key to this project is
being careful, controlled cutting and
no prying. Your knife is designed to
cut not pry.

Spheres within spheres

This is a variation on the ball in cage carving, where the cage is spherical instead of rectangular or cylindrical as in the other ball in cage projects in this book.

83.

As with a lot of what whittlers produce, people are very interested in these things, and its fun to make intricate stuff with a knife.

84.

85.

A 2x2 piece of knot free basswood about 10 inches long is a good start. Whittle it round.

Then whittle the end into a dome.

86.

87.

Measure down 2" or a tiny bit more and make a cut with a saw all the way around, but not through the wood. The saw is not absolutely necessary of course, but it does make things a little easier.

Whittle that end into a ball that is still attached to the rest of the stick which will serve as a handle and make the project easier to hold.

Sketch in some lines as shown.

Using those lines as a guide, put in some stop cuts, and clear out the wood in between them like this. Do this all around the sphere.

88.

With a sharp thin bladed knife undercut the "bands" and form the inner ball.

Keep going a little at a time from all sides. Don't do too much from one side. A little at a time from every side, and the job will get done.

There!

Once the basic project is done, it can be cut free of the extra "handle" part, and can be carried around in a jacket pocket to work on from time to time. If people see you doing this, or any other whittlin', you may be sure that a conversation will take place.

Here's one that is slightly more intricate, but really basically the same.

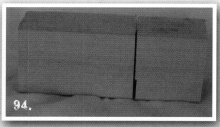

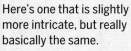

This time I cut the block with the saw before even rounding the 2x2, which could have been done for the previous one too.

Remember not to cut all the way through.

95.

Round the end.

96.

Turn it into a ball.

97.

Once the end has been made into a nice round ball, draw in the "cage" comprising the outer sphere.

98.

Make all of the drawing as even as possible

99.

Redraw if necessary. Regular pencil will work for you—felt pen shows up better in photos.

100.

Carefully make stop cuts along the lines and clear out the material between to reveal the inner ball.

101.

Work evenly around the whole thing.

102.

Whittle down far enough so that the inner ball does not have bumps on it. Remember to go all the way around and not to work away at one spot too long. This should be done evenly all the way around.

103.

Then it is time to undercut carefully with no prying.

104.

It will, of course, be necessary to free the entire project from the "handle" in order to do the one end properly.

105.

And there it is.

CHAPTER EIGHT
Fan Birds

People are totally mesmerized when a whittler uses his "wand" to make these birds. Some absolutely refuse to believe that it is possible to make them out of one piece of wood with no assembly until they are shown. The word "magic" has been used quite a bit when they are made.

Making fans out of wet wood, and birds and other items out of those fans, is an old craft that, as far as anybody knows, began in Russia many years ago. From there it spread to the Scandinavian countries and other parts of eastern Europe and then came to North America with Swedish and Norwegian loggers. Different carvers have their own styles, and some ways of doing these are peculiar to different regions. This is how I do them.

I often tell people that the first 100 of these birds are the hardest, and after that they are rather easy. I am not kidding. My first attempts were unspeakably hideous! I kept at it though and they got good enough that people started to pay me for them.

Payment is a special form of incentive that encouraged me to make still more.

The right wood is essential for this project. Fortunately, there are several kinds of wood that work well for this, and one of the best, Canadian spruce, is available in many parts of the world as construction lumber. I have personally seen Canadian spruce available in such diverse places as Arizona and Australia, so I know that it is possible to get it almost everywhere. I am sure other kinds of spruce will work well too.

If you are spruce hunting at a lumber yard or building supply store, it is helpful to be able to see the lumber piles in their plastic wrapper, because on that wrapper will be printed the location and name of the saw mill. Look for 2x8, 2x10, or 2x12 lumber from mills in British Columbia. Skip the 2x4 and 2x6 wood. Better wood is found in the larger sizes. Other wood may work too, but I know that the spruce from BC will work. The lumber will likely be stamped "SPF" which stands for spruce, pine and fir. There will be very little if any fir in the pile because Douglas fir is a premium building wood and gets a premium price. Pretty much the entire pile will be comprised of spruce and lodgepole pine. The pine will not be very good for the fans but the spruce will be great. How to tell the difference? Well, if the pile has just been unwrapped and not exposed to the sun and rain, the whitest wood will be the spruce. The pine will have a slightly yellow color to it. Do not depend upon the guidance of people who work in the large building supply places. They often do not know the difference. Pine will also have a, well, piney smell when cut and the spruce doesn't smell like much of anything recognizable except spruce.

There is a wood that grows in the eastern part of North America called white cedar that works very well for this. White pine, both eastern and western is good too. Yellow (or "Alaskan" though much of it is grown in BC) cedar is good too. Avoid western red cedar—it will be frustrating. Sugar pine works. Some pieces of lodgepole pine, Jack pine and Ponderosa pine work too but mostly are a problem especially for beginners.

In Australia I have used Huon pine (which isn't a pine), and King Billy (King William) pine. Avoid radiata pine.

Careful with the pines; there are at least 90 different kinds, 35 or so native to North America. Some are good to carve, and some are trouble. To say "pine" and expect something like say white pine, which is great to carve, is like saying "car" and expecting a Corvette. If a salesperson refers to "ordinary pine" they obviously have no idea about the subject. Seek advice elsewhere.

Try to find a board that has as few knots as possible. Look for straight and not wavy grain.

Cut a few pieces about 5 or 5½ inches long, and then split them out with an axe or hatchet in such a way that the growth rings run this way, and about this size. These birds can be made larger or smaller of course, but this is good size to start with.

These blanks of wood must be soaked in water for several days—a week is good. Put the split out blanks on end in a plastic container such as coffee comes in, put water in about half way up and put the lid on. If the wood is too tall or the lid is lost, pull a plastic bag over the open end and tuck it under the bottom. Let the container sit for a week and the wood will be ready to go. Once it has been soaked it can be kept for a long time in sealed plastic bags or containers with tight lids to prevent drying out. In warm weather mould will be a problem. Some alcohol sprinkled in the container helps, or the wood in their containers can be kept in the freezer.

Caution: excessive amounts of wood in the freezer can lead to domestic strife! Trust me on this.

Using a pencil mark out the lines as shown. Exact placement is not important, nor is the angle of that angled line. What is important is that the lines be at the same place on both sides of the little board.

Sketch the feather shape as shown on the edges of the blank as a guide.

Run a stop cut along the angled line (**Photo 6**) and whittle carefully with thumb push cuts toward that stop cut from the feather end of the blank (**Photo 7**). Do a little and then do a little on the other side of the blank until this result (**Photo 8**) is achieved. There should be about ⅛" of wood right in the middle all across the board.

It is important that no cuts go beyond the point indicated by the knife blade, down into that ⅛" of wood, which will become the hinge for spreading the feathers.

CLASSIC WHITTLING

Whittle the top end of the feather block to a
kind of blunt point. Also using the stop cut
and thumb push approach make the shallow
notches close to the feather block tip. Do this
evenly all the way across the board. Both sides
of the blank should be identical. Try to maintain
the same proportions as in **Photo 9**.

Notice that the feathers are tapered above
the hinge, but the part of the blank that will
become the bird's body is not bevelled or
tapered at all. This is left that way for now to
provide a good stop for the knife during the
splitting process.

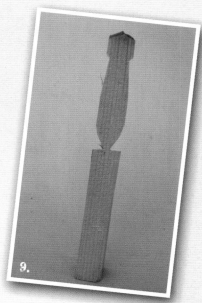

Bevel the little corners of
the notch near the tip of the
feather block.

Now comes the hardest part—splitting the
feathers. This is going to take some practice.
It is best if you lay aside your bird blank at this
point, keep it in plastic so that it won't dry out,
and get some of those other pieces of wood that
you soaked and practice splitting on six or seven
of them until you get this down a bit.

Some people find that it is easier to put their
wood in a vise for the splitting. I usually just put it
on a safe and solid surface, and hold the top of the
blank with my thumb as shown.

12.

Another view
of the process.

13.

Holding the blank this way (**Photo 13**) to split the feathers is **absolutely not** recommended!

Practice splitting feathers on wood that will not be used for an actual project before proceeding with your bird.

When you do get back to your blank you need to start on the side of the blank that will produce the shortest feathers (**Photo 14**).

Split all the way down to the shoulder that was left on the other side of the hinge.

Keep splitting until there is about this much left (**Photo 15**). There is no need to get any closer to your thumb.

14.

15.

16.

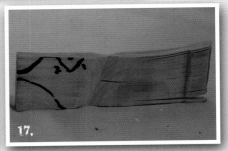

17.

After splitting the feathers, trim off the sharp shoulder, and work it down to a perfect "v" with no ridge on either side. Remember that no stop cuts can intrude into the hinge.

With the shortest feather on top sketch the bird's profile. Notice that two of the lines are numbered to indicate the order in which they are initially cut.

18.

This one is cut a little bit first forming a stop cut so that when # 2 is cut it won't split off a piece of wood including feathers.

19.

Work it down until it looks like this.

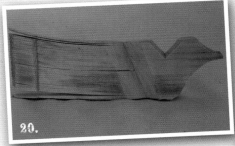

20.

Then shape the rest like this.

21.

Bevel the sharp corners and do a little chip carving for the eyes.

22.

Time to spread the feathers.

The top, shortest feather stays in the middle. The next feather is pulled out to one side. It doesn't matter which side, and twisted a bit so that it can be hooked to the first feather as shown.

23.

The next (3rd) feather is pulled to the other side, and hooked to the first feather.

24.

Go back to the other side and pull out and hook the next feather, and then to the other side, and so on.

When there are only a few feathers left (minimum of three), start over to form the tail.

25.

Pull the tail feathers down a bit as a group, and push the other feathers around a bit to even everything up

26.

A little bit of glue helps hold everything in place. I like to use cynoacrylate, which is a gap filling type of glue.

27.

And there it is.

Do another one soon. And then a few more, and they will start to look better. After a while they will look really good!

Another bird

Here is another way to do a bird, that is a little more involved, but results, I think, in a more realistic product.

28.

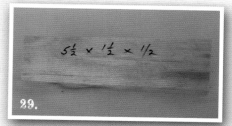

The starting point for this bird is very much the same as for the previous one. The same blank is used, with the rings oriented the same way, and of course, well soaked.

The layout is a little different though. On this one the longer feathers are going to be at the top of the blank, as shown.

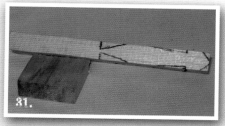

Here is the basic feather shape on the bottom edge of the blank.

Again, be very careful whittling down to the "hinge" so that no cuts extend down into it. I really need to emphasize this point. When/if you find that you are breaking off feathers when trying to spread them, it is often because of cuts intruding into the hinge fibers.

Leave the sharp, square "shoulder" at the point where the feather block attaches to the body (**Photo 33**). This will stop the knife blade as the feather splits are made.

A nice notch is needed to hook the feathers together. Bevel that sharp corner pointed out by the blade (**Photo 34**).

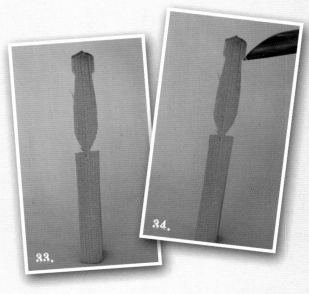

35.

36.

Now, starting with the short side of the feather block, start splitting the feathers, just like on the previous bird. If you have made several of the first bird whittlins there should be no problem making these.

Another look.

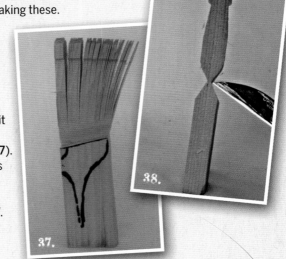

37.

38.

Split feathers until the last split is even with the back of the bird's neck as shown (**Photo 37**).

Bevel those sharp shoulders off now (**Photo 38**). They have served their purpose.

Take it down to a perfect "V".

Remember, no cuts beyond here.

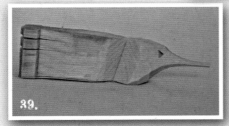

39.

40.

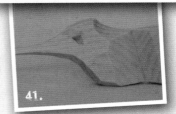

41.

Shape the bird's head, beak and body, and put in some eyes (**Photo 39**).

Break off that part behind the head that was not split into feathers (**Photo 40**).

Shape the back of the bird's head and neck (**Photo 41**).

Starting with the shortest feather, count off an odd number. I like to have seven feathers in my birds' tails, so because something often happens to a feather or two in the process, I count off nine feathers. The ninth one stays in the center, and the eighth one gets pulled out to one side and hooked over the ninth one.

Then the seventh feather gets pulled to the other side and hooked over the ninth one.

Keep going from side to side until there are seven feathers in the tail, or you have as many as you want, or can get out of the survivors!

There! The tail is formed.

Now take the next un-fanned feather, this would be feather ten, and pull it out all the way to an outside tail feather and hook it over. Then repeat on the other side, and just keep going.

Keep fanning feathers until there are no more or you run out of room, and pull out any leftovers. At first there probably won't be many, or even any, leftovers, but as you get better at splitting thin feathers you may need to thin them out as you make your birds.

When the fanning is completed the bird should look something like this.

 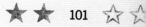

47.

Another view.

48.

Like so many of us, all this bird needs at this point is a slight chiropractic adjustment. Here is how to do that.

With the thumb and fingers of the left hand, firmly grasp the tail feathers on one side, and at the same time firmly grasp the wing feathers on the same side.

49.

Hold those tail feathers steady and twist down with the wing feathers.

50.

Like this.

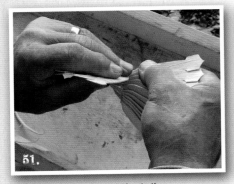

51.

Twist them right past the tail.

52.

It should look like this when you are done. The twist is on one side.

 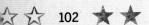

To do the other side of the bird, I flip the bird over and twist the other wing towards me, like this.

There.

Both wings are twisted (**Photos 55 and 55A**), and with a little shaping the bird is finished (**Photo 56**).

57.

58.

59.

Here are some more views of the finished bird.

I use a little glue at the hinge and where each feather touches the one next to it, to keep everything in place.

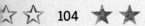

CHAPTER NINE
Human Faces

This project could get a whittler started in the fascinating art of caricature carving. It did it for me.

Many whittlers try faces, don't like the results and avoid human figures and faces from then on. They carve ducks, bears, chains, and spoons, anything but faces. Work through this, and you just might discover that you like human faces best of all!

In all of these projects, it is important to read and understand all of the instructions first and then come back and do them step by step. It is especially important with this one. Do it. It will save you trouble.

One of the main problems beginning face carvers encounter, is that their "people" all wind up with flat faces, and since real people do not have flat faces, they get discouraged.

One way to prevent that is to start carving the face by making or using a 90 degree corner. This simple approach will solve a lot of face carving problems, and is where we are going here.

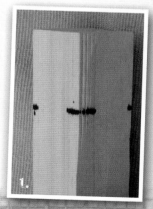

Start with a 2x2x6 or 7" piece of white pine, basswood, sugar pine or maybe even aspen. If the wood isn't square, whittle it square, and make it as close to square as possible. This will make it easier on down the line.

Mark a line about 2" down on one corner and then the same distance down on the other corners too.

2.

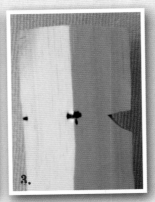

3.

4.

Choose one corner to be the one the nose will be on. This is where the whittlin' starts.

Use a stop cut at the line that was drawn and thumb push cuts to work up to that stop cut. Keep deepening the stop cut and taking more controlled clearing cuts until the block looks like this. Keep this as even as possible.

The view from the side. Try to keep the gap between the points, top and bottom, no more than ½ inch apart.

It might be helpful to use your pencil to mark this nose, an "N" seems appropriate.

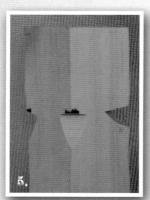

5.

6.

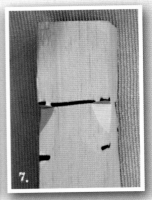

7.

Side view.

Time to do some more drawing. About ¼" down from the bottom of the nose notch draw another line. On the side corners draw lines that are just a little lower.

On the back corner draw a line that is lower still than the ones on the side corners.

 ★ ★ CLASSIC WHITTLING

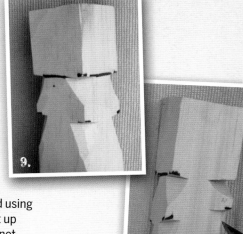

Make a stop cut under the nose and using only thumb push cuts, carefully cut up towards the nose. If these cuts are not controlled and careful, glue will be needed to put the nose back on. Not what we want. Be careful and save the glue.

Notice that the notch under the nose is not quite as deep as the one above it.

It is the same with the other corners. Don't make them quite as deep as the ones above them.

This is a back view (**Photo 9**).

The area indicated by the knife blade should be rounded, not flat from side to side (**Photo 10**).

This area can be fairly flat.

This notch (**Photo 12**) is not quite as deep as this notch (**Photo 13**).

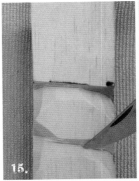

14.

15.

16.

Now, working only on the back join up the notches on the sides and back.

You can see that the hair of this figure is being formed.

Again, not as deep here (**Photo 15**) as here (**Photo 16**).

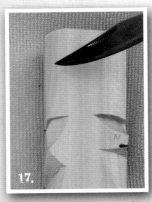

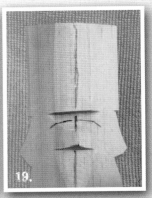

17.

18.

19.

Take a little time now and round up that square block at the top of this whittlin' that will become the hat.

It isn't going to be made totally round quite yet, but a start will be made.

Out comes the whittler's friend—the pencil—again, to draw a centerline first. Do not fail to do this. It will really help to keep everything lined up.

Then draw the eye lines, with just a little droop, too much and he will look sad. Angle the outside corners up and he will look angry! A lot can be done with eye angles.

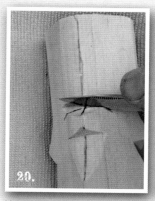

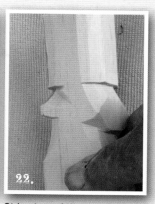

Use the eye lines as guides to make stop cuts right down into those little corners (**Photo 20**) and then take off the little corner underneath that stop cut with a carefully controlled clearing cut or two (**Photo 21**). It is better to make three or four tiny cuts that are controlled than one cut that is "almost" controlled.

Side view of the result.

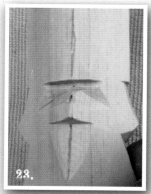

Do the same on the other side and make the two as much alike as possible.

OK, now it is time to do a really simple thing but it is kind of counter intuitive, and will require a look at this next photo and subsequent ones to get it.

At the top of the tip of the nose, make a cut that goes down and angles toward the mouth area. Right there at the point of the blade in the photo.

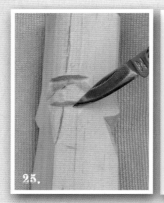

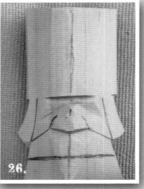

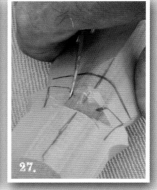

Then cut straight in under the nose at an angle from the center up to the side of the nose, on both sides. Study **Photo 25**, right at the point of the knife and in **Photo 26** too.

Put stop cuts alongside the nose on the lines that have been drawn. Take care to not undercut the nose. You will have to make an effort at this point. For some reason, the most natural thing to do when making these cuts is to undercut the sides of the nose. Don't do it.

See how my knife blade enters the wood in this shot. Do both sides of course.

Also in Photo 26, there are some guide lines drawn to help with the next few cuts. The outsides of the nostrils are sketched in. Always make noses bigger than you think they should be. They have a way of getting smaller as they are worked on, so start big. Notice that these lines for the nose are not straight up and down, but angled up in the direction of the bridge of the nose.

The lines that mark the hairline up the sides of the figure's face are also not straight up and down and are slightly curved. There are very few straight lines in nature and parallel lines are even more rare. If you see these (straight an/or parallel lines) showing up on your faces, you know that something is wrong.

You will, of course, notice that I have drawn in some straight lines to mark out the moustache in apparent defiance of my previous sentence. Those lines are temporary and the moustache will be rounded up later.

Observe that the top of the moustache line is from the corner of the nose to the lower hair notch. The bottom moustache line is making for a pretty wide moustache. This is by design. Skinny moustaches are for later in your whittlin' career. They tend to break.

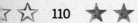

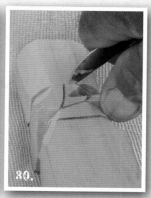

Stop cut along the line that forms the top of the moustache (**Photo 28**) and along the hairline. (**Photo 29**).

Make a little stop cut along the underside of the hat at the top of our guy's temples, like this.

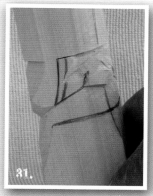
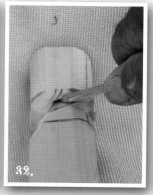
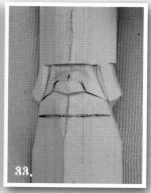

See how I have drawn a line alongside the figure's face to show where some wood needs to be cleared out.

This is the cut. I removed the thumb that would be pushing this cut so that it could be observed.

Do both sides. Don't be afraid to cut right through the eye sockets.

See the little crescent marks above the moustache on both sides? That is where some wood needs to be removed forming the cheeks and the top of the moustache.

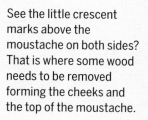
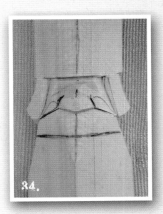

35.

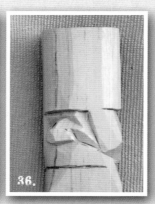

36.

37.

To actually take that wood out, since the stop cuts alongside the nostrils and the top of the moustache have already been made, cut down towards the moustache stop cut.

Photo 36 shows the result of these cuts.

Bevel off the top of the moustache now by taking off the sharp corner of the moustache, by cutting from the tip of the moustache toward the nose. Thumb push cut here lest you cut off the nose!

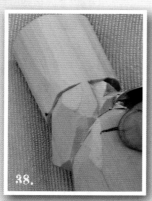

38.

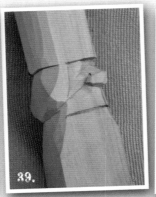

39.

40.

A little downward cut at the junction of the nose and moustache will clean this up.

The result.

Now we will start on the underside of the moustache. Begin with a good stop cut along this line

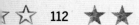

41.

42.

43.

Then whittle up towards the moustache with controlled cuts and relieve the area under the moustache on both sides.

Keep that area under the moustache rounded (**Photo 42**). We want to avoid the look of a flat face.

Do not go deeper in this area than you went here (**Photo 43**).

44.

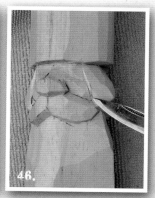

45.

46.

You can see that there has been a little drawing done to help give that moustache a slightly more realistic shape.

Here half of the carving has been done to shape the bottom of the moustache. It doesn't look so blocky now.

Take a little bit out of the corner formed by the hair and the moustache to round up the cheeks a bit. Cut, do not "dig" or "chew" this out.

In this photo I have also started to trim the hair a bit under the hat. You know that when you put a hat on, your hair gets squished down to nothing between your head and the hat. That is what we want to depict.

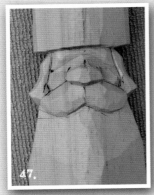
47.

48.

49.

Round up the underside of the moustache too.

Here is where we are at this point.

Another view.

Here we have a view of the back.

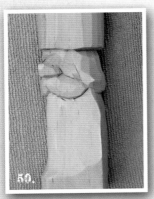
50.

Here you can see that some more of the beard has been whittled again with controlled cuts toward the moustache. This is a good place for that cut where the hat area of this piece would be against your chest. Your non-knife fingers are holding the end of the beard, the knife is pinched and the hand contacts your body before the blade does. These cuts can be very precise.

51.

Notice here the sides of the beard. I have not cut off the sides, so the beard seems to flare out. Here is a case where if you didn't read these instructions first you probably already made the beard rather narrow, which works too.

I like to avoid parallel lines on faces, and here the sides of the beard are not parallel. I think that this gives the piece a more lifelike appearance.

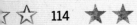

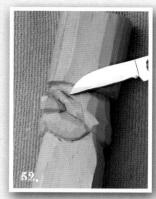

Extend those eye sockets a bit more to kind of come around the side of the face as shown.

Also cut some really thin slits to make it look like this guy has really squinty eyes. You will get to carving eyes sometime, but not today.

Since the hair was whittled down some to depict the squished down hair, there is room to further round the hat block.

Draw a line all around the hat block as shown. The area under that line will become the brim, and the area above will become the crown of an exaggerated top hat.

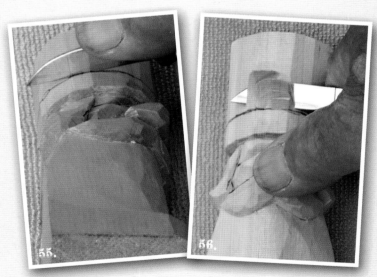

Make a stop cut on that brim line (**Photo 55**), and whittle down towards it (**Photo 56**).

Repeat all the way around the hat.

Try to make the hat fit the head that it is on.

For example, the indicated part of the crown (**Photo 57**) should line up with the forehead, and so on all the way around the head (**Photo 58**).

At this point we can shape the brim of the hat, first by scooping out a bit at the front (**Photo 59**) and at the back (**Photo 60**).

Now start rounding up the sides of the brim by trimming the bottom edge, and a little at the top. Only one side has been done here so that you can see the progression.

To make a mouth on this guy, if you want one, just make a couple of stop cuts right in at that inverted "V" in the center of the moustache.

Then cut across the grain and take the chip out and form the mouth. Keep this small, so that the absence of teeth does not become a factor. Teeth are fun too, but that is for another day.

You may want to work on his nose a bit more too to make it more, well, "nosey". Looking at your own face in the mirror can help here. You could take a close look at those around you too, but unless they are whittlers too, you might get some funny looks, and comments—"What are you looking at?"

  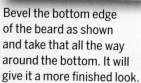

Bevel the bottom edge of the beard as shown and take that all the way around the bottom. It will give it a more finished look.

Here are a few more views of the finished product.

Here I have relieved the area below the lip by cutting down from it.

Well there's a start in the wonderful world of human caricature. Like other forms of whittlin' this can be quite addictive.

Once you get a handle on whittlin' human faces, you can then create a walking stick with personality.

Walking sticks

Walking sticks, canes, hiking stick/staves are a whole category of whittlin' in itself. Good walking sticks can be made out of dozens, maybe hundreds of different kinds of trees and bushes. Everybody can find material somewhere for free. The sky is the limit as to what gets whittled into/onto the stick too.

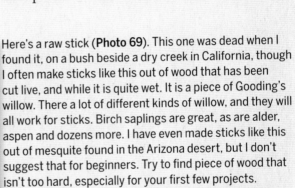

Here is how to use the things learned in the previous section on the simple human face, and create a really unique stick.

At some points in these instructions it will be helpful to flip back to that previous section for some of the details on making a face.

Here's a raw stick (**Photo 69**). This one was dead when I found it, on a bush beside a dry creek in California, though I often make sticks like this out of wood that has been cut live, and while it is quite wet. It is a piece of Gooding's willow. There a lot of different kinds of willow, and they will all work for sticks. Birch saplings are great, as are alder, aspen and dozens more. I have even made sticks like this out of mesquite found in the Arizona desert, but I don't suggest that for beginners. Try to find piece of wood that isn't too hard, especially for your first few projects.

Notice that this one was about 2½" thick, and that in stickmaking I always put the thick end up. Later when I finish the work, I will taper the stick from the top to the bottom. You never want to have the heaviest part of a walking stick closest to the ground. The fewer little branches the better, because every little branch is a knot and they will create problems when you try to whittle the face. Also avoid cracked wood. Stay away from driftwood too, unless you really like sharpening, because driftwood is usually full of grit which will take the edge right off of your knife.

Decide where on the stick that you would like the face, and draw a centerline vertically (**Photo 70**). A line depicting the underside of the hat has also been drawn on this one. Use a regular pencil, the marker was used to show up better in the photos.

The hat line goes right around the back.

In the chapter on whittlin' the simple face, the work was done on the corner of the block to avoid the dreaded "flat face effect" which often afflicts whittlers of the human form. Since this stick did not come with a corner, it is necessary to make one. Under the hat line and on both sides of the center line, whittle off two flat spots that almost come together at about a 90 degree angle. Leave a tiny flat tip, just enough to retain the centerline. It doesn't matter how far down the stick these flats go. They should not intrude up into the hat though.

Let's start on the nose. Use a stop cut under the center front of the hat brim line, and then carefully whittle up to it, clearing out the area above the nose.

Don't make the gap too big unless you want a really long nose on your figure.

In this photo, the area under the nose has been relieved, remember, not quite as deeply as the area under the hat brim, and the sides and back of the head under the hat brim have been relieved also.

76.

Some guiding lines have been added.

77.

Don't forget to put in a good center line.

78.

79.

Here the underside of the hair has been cleared out all the way around, including the back (**Photos 78** & **79**).

80.

81.

Now on one side the hair line along the face has been removed (**Photos 80** & **81**).

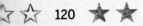

Both sides of the face/hair line have been done, and the moustache block has been drawn, as well as the eye lines and the outside of the nose.

The eye notch is done on one side.

The other eye notch and the cheek are done.

Time to do the underside of the moustache.

Be careful to avoid flattening things here, or going too deep.

Here the mouth and lip have been added and the moustache has been shaped up. Notice the finishing work on the hair on one side too.

88.

89.

A closer look.

See how the hair is worked down? Only half done here.

90.

91.

92.

On a hiking stick, I like to whittle a smooth place to grip the staff, just under the beard **(Photo 90)**, making a smooth transition from the beard, and making that grip a little narrower at the top where the thumb and forefinger go around it **(Photo 91)**. Keep trying it with your hand, and whittlin' a bit until it feels right.

This stick has great bark, so I decided to leave some on. I worked the notch above the brim down in such a way to leave bark on the brim, but also give some shape to it. Remember to not go too deep with this notch. Remember that the hat should fit the head that it is on.

Taper the crown of the hat from as high up as you are going to go, down toward the brim. Small, carefully controlled cuts are the key here, to avoid chopping off the brim.

96.

97.

And there he is!

I did carve eyes in this one, but that is a subject for at least another chapter, and probably part of another book.

98.

Here is a comfortable and useful walking stick, with personality.

CHAPTER TEN
Finishing

There is always a little sadness when the project, a whittlin' or a book, comes close to the end. It's over!

Sometimes it feels good that it's over, especially if there have been some problems along the way, but for me somehow, the magic is in the unfolding of the work, and when that is done, well, its done. Of course there is more wood out there.

There is another meaning to "finishing" too, having to do with substances and processes that are applied to the work to complete and preserve it.

Most of my whittlins get no application of anything other than handling, which does develop a patina on the pieces after a time. To me that is one of the attractions of whittlin'—just use the knife and "there!" Not everything needs a finish.

Sometimes, though, it is better to use sandpaper to obtain a smooth finish. Walking sticks for example, that are made out of wood with a really nice grain, like Rocky Mountain juniper, benefit from sanding to show off that nice grain. Mostly I try to avoid sandpaper. It is the "S" word in my classes. I think it detracts from the whittled look.

Equally important when showing off nice grain or color, is to use something to further bring out those features. You can use boiled linseed oil (not raw), Danish oil, or any number of products that are available. In my experience, the water based clear finishes "kill" or deaden the color and grain and so I don't use them.

Some woods, like cherry and juniper are very sensitive to ultra violet light and their color will fade badly if some kind of UV inhibiting finish is not used. There are deck oils that have UV inhibiters mixed in them. You local paint store will help with this. Ask in more than one place. Sometimes excellent products are available from one store and seemingly totally unknown by others.

Shoe polish is a simple and kind of traditional finish for whittlins. It is available in various shades and colors. Just apply it like you would to shoes. It will darken the little crevices and give them an antique look.

Seeing whittlins, particularly walking sticks, finished with glossy varnish just drives me nuts! Please help me with my mental health and avoid them.

I do sometimes paint my whittlins, and when I do, as in the case of caricatures, I dip them into boiled linseed oil, or brush it on if that is more convenient, let it soak in for a while and then mop up the excess with a rag or paper towel. Spread out these rags or paper towels to let them dry. Do not bunch them up or pile them up as they can develop enough heat to spontaneously ignite! I let the oil dry for at least a day and then I use acrylic artist's paints, thinned radically to allow the wood grain to show through. I do not want my whittlins to look like plastic.

Spoons and other kinds of treen, which will be used for food preparation or consumption, can be used without a finish. Recent research has proved that wooden utensils, unfinished, or finished with food grade mineral oil or walnut oil, is more hygienic than plastic. Actually the bare wood was best in the research. I have boiled some spoons and ladles in beeswax and they have performed excellently. Never put treen or any other wood item in a dishwasher.

I often say, that I am just producing designer firewood anyway, so don't be afraid to experiment, with your whittlin' or in the finishing of it.

You know, one of the really great things about this craft is that it is all about getting busy and doing something with simple tools and materials.

So don't just sit there! Wave that magic wand—whittle!

About the author

Rick Wiebe has been whittling for almost 60 years, and still has a full complement of working fingers.

He carves many different kinds of projects, walking sticks with animal heads, human caricatures, and large log projects using chainsaws and more.

His pieces are in private collections worldwide.

Rick teaches whittling and carving to children aged nine and up and adults too, in many different venues including clubs, schools, homeschool groups, community recreation programs, and private sessions.

Rick is also the author of *Whittlin' Whistles*, published in 2012 by Linden Publishing.

He and his wife of 46 years live in Westbank, BC, and work with Mobile Missionary Assistance Program (mmap.org) in the southern US during the winter. He often gets to carve as part of this work too.

Rick and Helen sell carving tools at woodcarvingbiz.com where a gallery of some of his work can be seen.

More Great Woodworking Books from Linden Publishing

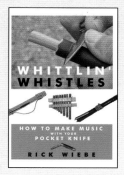

Whittlin' Whistles:
How to Make Music with Your
Pocket Knife
64 pp. $12.95 / 978-1-610350-49-5

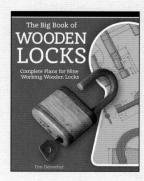

The Big Book of Wooden Locks
152 pp. $24.95
978-1-610352-22-2

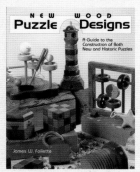

New Wood Puzzle Designs
96 pp. $21.95
978-0-941936-57-6

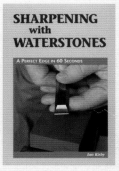

Sharpening with Waterstones:
A Perfect Edge in 60 Seconds
96 pp. $14.95
978-0-941936-76-7

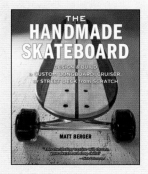

The Handmade Skateboard
160 pp. $24.95
978-1-940611-06-8

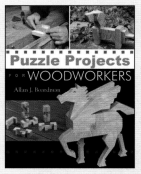

Puzzle Projects for Woodworkers
96 pp. $19.95
978-1-933502-11-3

More Great Woodworking Books From Linden Publishing

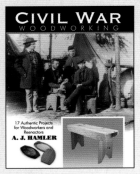

Civil War Woodworking
164 pp. $24.95
978-1-933502-28-1

The Art of Whittling
91 pp. $9.95
978-1-933502-07-6

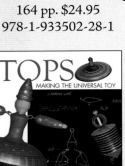

Tops: Making the Universal Toy
128 pp. $17.95
978-1-933502-17-5

Carving for Kids
104 pp. $16.95
978-1-933502-02-1

Handmade Furniture
120 pp. $19.95
978-1-610352-10-9

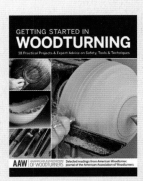

Getting Started in Woodturning
224 pp. $27.95
978-1-940611-09-9